THE PONTIFICAL COUNCIL FOR THE FAMILY

MARRIAGE AND FAMILY

THE PONTIFICAL COUNCIL FOR THE FAMILY

Marriage and Family

Experiencing the Church's
Teaching in Married Life

IGNATIUS PRESS   SAN FRANCISCO

Title of the Italian original:
Matrimonio e Famiglia: Dottrina e Vita;
Problemi, orientamenti, esperienze
© 1987 Editrice Elle di Ci, Torino

Cover by Riz Boncan Marsella

With ecclesiastical approval
© 1989 Ignatius Press, San Francisco
All rights reserved
ISBN 0-89870-218-6
Library of Congress catalogue number 88-81273
Printed in the United States of America

CONTENTS

Preface   9

Address to the Third Plenary Assembly
   of the Pontifical Council for the Family,
   by His Holiness John Paul II   11

Part One
Presentations

Conscience, Truth, and Magisterium in Conjugal
   Morality, by Msgr. Carlo Caffarra   21

Union and Procreation in Marriage and Conjugal
   Life, by Msgr. Francisco Gil Hellín   37

Human Difficulties and Clarifications of the
   Church's Magisterium on Conjugal Life,
   by Wladyslaw Bernard Skrzydlewski, O.P.   51

Doctrine and Method in the Preparation of and Action
   by Workers in the Pastoral Care of Marriage,
   by Wanda and Andrzej Półtawski   67

Part Two
Reports

Medical Personnel and Natural Family Planning,
   by John and Lorna Bergin   87

Transmission of Apostolic Sensitivity Inside
   and Outside the Home, by Roberto and
   Elizabeth De La Fuente   99

CONTENTS

Presentation and Reception of the Holy Father's Catechesis, by Bernard and Huguette Fortin — 105

Dissemination of the Pope's Catechesis: Its Publication, Reception, and Problems, by Norbert and Renate Martin — 113

The Pope's Catechesis on "The Transmission of Life": "Our Mission to Love and Understand the Truth of Life in the Face of Official Propaganda", by Alfred and Marie Mignon Mascarenhas — 121

Continence and Freedom in Conjugal Self-Giving, by Richard and Barbara McBride — 135

Fertility Awareness and Education for Chastity, by Jean-Marie and Anouk Meyer — 143

The Rights of the Family and Social Powers, by Luís Alberto and María del Coro Petit Herrera — 147

Living a Christian Marriage, by Ron and Mavis Pirola — 155

The Christian Family at the Service of Reconciliation, by Rodolfo and María Valdes — 165

Children: Contribution to the Good of the Family, by Marijo and Darka Zivkovic — 173

ABBREVIATIONS

AAS: *Acta Apostolicae Sedis*

CCL: *Corpus Christianorum*, Series Latina

CG: *Contra Gentiles*

FC: *Familiaris Consortio*

GS: *Gaudium et Spes*

HV: *Humanae Vitae*

RH: *Redemptor Hominus*

PREFACE

In this book, we are offering to all who are interested in the pastoral care of the family the major papers and reports delivered at the Third Plenary Assembly of the Pontifical Council for the Family. From December 11 to 15, 1985, the twenty married couples who are members of the Pontifical Council and the Presidential Committee met in the offices of the Council in Rome in Palazzo San Calisto.

The main theme of this assembly was: "John Paul II's Catechesis on *Humanae Vitae*". In the discourse which the Holy Father addressed to the Pontifical Council for the Family on December 13, the dual doctrinal/pastoral aspect underlying the various reports was carefully analyzed. The Pope's words, which are reproduced at the beginning of this book, are the best introduction to the work of the assembly and the guidelines drawn up by it. The Holy Father insists on fidelity to the doctrine of the Magisterium on marriage and the family, and on promoting pastoral activities which will make these truths known and help Christians incorporate them into their lives. For this reason, the title of this book is: *Marriage and Family: Experiencing the Church's Teaching in Married Life.*

The papers by Professors Carlo Caffarra, Francisco Gil Hellín, Wladyslaw Bernard Skrzydlewski, and Drs. Wanda and Andrzej Póltawski contain the following main points respectively. The Church's Magisterium serves the conscience of the faithful by guaranteeing truth in moral requirements. The morality of conjugal life is not an arbitrary requirement: the unitive and procreative meanings of the spouses' intimate life are postulated by the very essence of marriage. Despite the difficulties that exist, spouses' fidelity to the doctrine of the Magisterium is a source of human and Christian richness. In the training and activities of family pastoral workers, the entire truth must be presented without misleading omissions, and all appropriate methods and techniques must be used in order to transmit these values and foster their assimilation.

The couple members of the Council also gave reports, based on their own experiences and reflections, on some specific aspects of the pastoral care of marriage. These different initiatives illustrate the numerous possibilities that are offered by pastoral care of marriage in complete fidelity to the Church's Magisterium.

In sending these texts from the assembly to the press, I would like to encourage and hearten all those married couples who are aware of the dignity of that sacrament which makes them participants in the spousal union between Christ and the Church.

Discovering the divine power that enlivens the Christian family's human existence will help couples be strong in the face of the real difficulties that arise in living the requirements of the Faith. Furthermore, they will put the apostolic meaning of the family into practice and make it known to many other families by creating the "domestic Church" in their home.

> Edouard Cardinal Gagnon
> President of the Pontifical Council
> for the Family

ADDRESS TO THE THIRD PLENARY ASSEMBLY OF THE PONTIFICAL COUNCIL FOR THE FAMILY

December 13, 1985

HIS HOLINESS JOHN PAUL II

Your Eminence,
Dear Brothers and Sisters,

1. I am happy to receive you on the occasion of your general assembly, which is a high point in the activity of your Council particularly because of the contributions of the family members who have come from all parts of the globe.

We have just finished the Extraordinary Synod held on the occasion of the twentieth anniversary of the closing of Vatican Council II. Together with the presidents of the Episcopal Conferences and the other Synod Fathers, we have sought to evaluate its spiritual fruits and renew our desire to be docile to the action of the Holy Spirit, who stimulates his Church to be increasingly aware of the mystery of its identity, through Christ, and of the responsibility which falls upon it before the world and contemporary men.

For the past month we have been commemorating various conciliar documents which were approved and published exactly twenty years ago. One of the principal documents was the Pastoral Constitution *Gaudium et Spes*, which was adopted on December 7, 1965. It presents a Christian vision of man and of society, and the interaction of the Church as the people of God with human communities. It deals with many problems which are of crucial importance for today's world, and, of primary import, the doctrine concerning marriage and the family must be mentioned. Since that time, these two subjects have been the object of special attention by the Church's Magisterium. The Encyclical *Humanae Vitae* of my predecessor Paul VI, the Synod on the mission of the family, and the Apostolic Exhortation *Familiaris Consortio*, as well as the catechesis which I dedicated to concrete aspects of Christian doctrine on marriage—without counting the many pastoral documents of my brother bishops—have pointed out to the faithful the correct human and Christian order of that union which makes them share in the sacramental mystery of marriage.

The Committee for the Family—which became the Pontifical Council for the Family—was created in order to contribute better to presenting and disseminating the doctrine on marriage and the family, and to bring direct and appropriate assistance to the specific pastoral care of various situations which affect family life. Therefore, you are—all of you who are full members of this department of the Church—co-workers with the Pope in his concern for all the Churches. I sincerely thank you for your collaboration. Your mission concerns both the doctrine and the pastoral care of families.

2. Thus, first of all, you must make reference to the truth which the Church presents and transmits concerning marriage. The Church's Magisterium does not create the doctrine: it teaches the requirements of the moral order so that, in its light, the judgment of conscience can be true. The

faithful have the right to receive teaching about moral truth from the Magisterium. And it cannot be said that the Church's Magisterium is opposed to the "rights of conscience". If human reason and the Magisterium based on revelation have access, though in different ways, to truth which is based on God, conscience enlightened by reason will not, in that other light which comes to it through the Magisterium, see merely one concept among others but the support given by divine Providence to our human nature in its weak and limited condition.

Therefore, the Church's Magisterium does not replace people's moral conscience. It helps it to be formed, to discover the truth about things, the mystery and vocation of the human person, the profound meaning of his actions and relations. Thus conscience can never give way to acting arbitrarily. It can err by orienting itself toward what reasonably seems to be something good, but its duty is to orient itself toward the good according to truth.

It is not surprising that marriage and conjugal relations are one of the areas where internal disorder—a consequence of original sin and of each one's personal sins—has widely spread the fog of bewilderment and doubt. It is precisely one point where the Church's Magisterium must present the truth while being particularly attentive to promoting the good of people and of human society, which is so closely dependent on this basic unit, the family.

In presenting the moral laws which surround the truth of the spouses' gift, not only does the Church promote the moral rectitude of each of the spouses; she defends the truth about marriage itself, the origin and guarantee of the family. For this reason, the Pastoral Constitution *Gaudium et Spes*, in presenting the objective criteria "based on the nature of the human person and his acts" which determine the morality of the spouses' intimate life, calls them "objective standards . . . which preserve the full sense of mutual self-giving and human procreation in the context of true love" (no. 51). At the same time, this mutual self-giving and human procreation are none other in conjugal life than a faithful reflection of the nature of marriage. Logically, the basic links between the nature of marriage itself, the mutual self-giving, and openness to life determine the truth about the specific acts of marriage while conditioning whether they are good or not.

In this sense, it can be said that the call of the Church's doctrine is a profound way of practicing charity: a love which is not limited to providing "solutions", perhaps easy ones which are immediately effective, but which, like a good doctor, seeks to take care of the causes of the disorder even if, at times, the results cannot be seen immediately. Wherever disorder in conjugal life abounds, the foundations of the institution of marriage and the stability of the family are undermined, and profound remedies, depending on the nature of the disorder, must be prepared.

It is necessary to present the doctrine well with arguments and examples capable of moving and convincing our contemporaries. Furthermore, the problems of the family are far from being limited to those I have just mentioned concerning the spouses' union. They are many. They concern not only procreation but education and the entire family environment.

Finally, scientific advances, especially those concerning the embryo, are now raising many new and serious questions. The Church must face up to these. Your Council has its part in this and must be careful always to allow the complex responses of the Magisterium be the fruit of collaboration by several departments and to use the reflection of highly qualified experts as well as the theological and moral judgment of diverse theologians and their pastors. This is still another service which the Church must offer to consciences and to society.

3. The apostolic activity of your Council, based on doctrine, should aim at a better pastoral care of the family, which will enable the faithful to accept this truth in a better way and make it enter into their own lives as well as into the morals of society. This is the second aspect of your mission, which is inseparable from the first one. You have also reflected during your assembly on the way to prepare workers for the pastoral care of the family.

Your contribution remains very valuable and special, for you are within the Curia, in direct relationship with the Pope. The scope of your concern is the universal Church. The very composition of your Council, with Christian couples from different countries who have assimilated the Church's teaching on the family and strive to live it, favors such an apostolate.

But you are also aware of the immensity of this task. All of the laity living their vocation of marriage are called to this apostolate, aided by their priests. It is hoped that many initiatives will be made of this type in the local churches and that family associations, movements, and specialized centers will offer qualified and generous collaboration inspired by the Christian spirit and faithful to the doctrine of the Church. On the local scene, the bishops are directly responsible for the Christian authenticity and the appropriateness of such activity. They are counting on your understanding and encouragement.

This apostolate will take into consideration the education and particular situations of persons in order to lead them to greater understanding of the requirements of Christian marriage and to progress in conjugal and parental love, as the Lord desires. If it is not permissible to speak about the "graduality of the law", as if the law were more or less demanding according to concrete situations, it is no less necessary to take into consideration "the law of graduality" (cf. *FC*, no. 34). For every good pedagogue, without invalidating the principles, is attentive to the personal situation of those with whom he is dealing in order to enable them to be more receptive to the truth. Those whose lives conform to these requirements, or who at least strive to live them consistently, are in a better position to communicate these values. In addition to this Christian consistency with the truth, all the sciences related to pedagogy, those which help in knowing the person better and favor communication, will certainly be of great use.

But even though this task of doctrinal formation is so necessary, the witness of Christian spouses' lives has unique value. The Church's Magisterium does not present truths which are impossible to be lived. Of course, the requirements of Christian life surpass man's possibilities if he is not helped by grace. But those who let themselves be enlivened by God's Spirit have the experience that fulfillment of Christ's law is possible and that "my yoke is easy, and my burden light" (Mt 11:30), and such faithfulness brings great benefits. The witness of this experience thus constitutes for other couples of goodwill, who are often disoriented and dissatisfied, a powerful theme of credibility and attraction. Like the salt, of which the Gospel speaks, it gives them a taste for living in this way. The sacrament of marriage makes Christian couples capable of this charism (cf. *FC*, no. 5; also homily for the opening of the Sixth Synod of Bishops, *AAS*, 72 [1980], p. 1008). They show that Christian values crown and strengthen human values. The full truth about Christ, far from belittling real love, guarantees it and protects it. It is at the source of the spouses' own good. It engenders for society couples who will be the leaven of a better society.

Many of those in charge of civil society who are aware of the profound changes and of the crisis which so widely affect family life, the stability of couples, and the happiness of spouses and children will undoubtedly take into consideration the importance of this specific contribution, which is inspired by natural and Christian moral principles and offered loyally and humbly.

Here, in any case, is what we must promote in the Church with clarity and courage in liaison with the living forces already working for the pastoral care of the family.

The next Synod, on the mission of the laity, will undoubtedly strengthen this awareness and appeal, which have already been enlivened by the preceding ordinary Synod, because the family is one of the specific areas in which it is up to the laity to fill society with the Spirit of Christ.

I would like to thank you once again for your special service to the Church within the framework of the Pontifical Council for the Family. I hope it will be increasingly fruitful.

I entrust your work to God as well as the intentions dearest to your hearts, especially the happiness and radiance of your families—and I affectionately greet your children—and also the difficult situations of the families whose distress you know and who are counting on you. I wish you the peace and joy of Christmas as I grant you my Apostolic Blessing.

Part One

PRESENTATIONS

CONSCIENCE, TRUTH, AND MAGISTERIUM IN CONJUGAL MORALITY

MSGR. CARLO CAFFARRA

Before going into the particular topic which has been given to me, I think it is necessary to make some general remarks about moral conscience and its relationship to the Church's moral Magisterium. This will be the first part of my reflection. In the second part, I will take up the specific theme.

1. MORAL CONSCIENCE AND THE CHURCH'S MORAL MAGISTERIUM (General Reflections)

I would like to begin by pointing out some reasons which have made the problem of the relationship between conscience and Magisterium "difficult" both with regard to thought and on the practical level.

First. This had already been pointed out by J. H. Newman in very strong terms:

> Its miserable counterfeit . . . the very right and freedom of conscience to dispense with conscience . . . the right of thinking, speaking, writing, and acting, according to their judgement or their humour, without any thought of God at all . . . (*Letter to the Duke of Norfolk,* in *Difficulties of Anglicans,*

II, p. 250). Deference to the law of conscience . . . is easily perverted into a kind of self-confidence, namely a deference to our judgement (*Oxford University Sermons,* p. 172).

Thus, the first cause is due to the *equivocalness* attached to the term of *moral conscience*. It is used with two meanings which are contradictory to one another and irreconcilable. Let us take a look at them. This very serious situation requires us first of all to make an effort at rigorously clarifying the concept of moral conscience.

Second. A confusion of terms always indicates a confusion of concepts. Such confusion creates a serious problem since *facilius ad veritatem pervenitur ab errore quam a confusione* [it is easier to reach truth from error than from confusion] (St. Thomas Aquinas). What causes this confusion? Basically by exchanging (or, namely, confusing) the affirmation—on which we should reflect at length—whereby the moral obligation arises in the conscience and *through* the conscience with the affirmation that the moral obligation arises *from* the conscience; in confusing the *manifesting* function (of the truth), which belongs to the conscience, with the *constitutive* function (of the truth), which, as we will see, cannot *in any way* be attributed to man's moral conscience. This situation requires us to make an effort to clarify as much as possible the precise function of moral conscience in moral life, especially with regard to the truth about what is right.

Third. The problem is transferred from the relationship between moral conscience and political authority—which, since the formation of absolutist states, has continued being a great problem in modern political philosophy—to the relationship between moral conscience (of the believer) and the Church's Magisterium without any change at all. That is to say, the following proportion is set up: moral conscience (of the citizen) : political authority = moral conscience (of the believer) : Church's Magisterium. This fact requires us to discover the *specific quality*, the *originality* of the relationship between conscience and the Magisterium, which is *not in any way* reducible to the former type of relationship.

In this way we have indicated the two main themes with which we will deal in the first part of our reflection.

1.1 The nature of moral conscience and its relationship to the truth about what is right

Moral conscience, despite the fact that the word makes us think of a faculty of our spirit, is really an *act* of our reason, a judgment through which I discover moral truth, the truth about what is right or wrong ("an instrument for detecting moral truth wherever it lies hid", J. H. Newman, *Oxford University Sermons*, p. 66). These simple words hide, or better, attempt to describe one of the most awesome and mysterious events that can take place in our spirit.

Let us begin immediately by saying that through this act—which precisely makes up conscience—man does not discover just any moral truth but a truth inherent in the action which he is about to perform (or has performed). It is a truth which concerns the person in his individuality, as the subject about to perform an action. Conscience makes him *know* precisely the moral truth about *this action*: that is, its moral goodness or evil. At this point it is logical for us to ask: How can he know this truth? How is this judgment which makes up moral conscience created? An entire concept of conscience ultimately depends on the answer to this question.

We must start from the observation, based on our daily experience, that *this* judgment has a force all its own: that of absolutely obligating, and not only hypothetically, our decisions and our freedom. Thus, it is so clear for each person that speaking of "conscience" and "feeling obligated to . . ." are almost the same thing. But what is of greatest interest is to take note of and to understand the nature and the unique form of this obligation.

In fact it is certain that, in one sense, every judgment of our reason requires a certain behavior and, therefore, certain decisions of the will. If we know that a certain food is harmful to our health, we usually decide to avoid it. If we know that the weather outside is bad and we decide to go out, we logically decide to dress appropriately. And so on. Nevertheless these and other judgments of our reason require a coherent behavior but only *hypothetically. If* you want to be healthy, knowing that a certain food . . . If you do not want to get bronchitis, knowing that the weather . . . But if we pay attention to the judgment of the conscience, we see that the obligation generated by it is basically of a different nature. That obligation does not depend on an "if": it does not depend on anything. It is imposed immediately by itself on man's freedom. Conscience speaks *absolutely*: you must do this, you must not do that. The voice of conscience places man's freedom before an absolute: an absolute duty.

We, therefore, have an inner situation which is unique. On one hand, only in the face of *this* judgment, that of the conscience, does freedom feel absolutely obliged. On the other hand, this judgment is an act *of* the individual, of the subject, and only *his*. How can it happen that the person through one of *his* own actions feels interiorly obliged so deeply and so strictly as not to be able, with a contrary action, to be released? It is an action of his—an act of *his* reason—which has bound his freedom. With an act—an act of *his* reason—he is released. The reality of our inner experience clearly attests to us that this does not happen. Man cannot excuse himself from the duty to which the judgment of conscience obliges him. The universal experience of remorse demonstrates this. This impossibility forces us to a deeper reflection about moral conscience.

The fact that man feels he cannot excuse *himself* from the obligation of his own conscience shows that its judgment makes the person know about a truth that exists before conscience itself. This is a truth that is not real because of the strength of our conscience or because our conscience knows it, but, on the contrary, our conscience knows it because that truth exists. In brief: truth does not depend on conscience but conscience depends on truth. What truth? The truth in the light of which and on the strength of which "this action is good and to be performed" or "this action is illicit and to be avoided". Thus we have already arrived at this very important conclusion: since man is obliged only by the judgment of his own conscience (auto-nomy), and since the judgment of his own conscience obligates because it makes the truth known, *thus* man is autonomous when subjected to the truth. One's own autonomy consists of one's subordination to the truth.

Now we must briefly return to reflecting on the truth known through the judgment of our own conscience. What truth is this? Because conscience is a judgment concerning our action from a moral standpoint, it is a *practical* truth (concerning human action), a truth about the good and evil of our actions. The judgment of our conscience uncovers in the action I am about to perform (or have performed)—or due to its make-up or the circumstances in which it is performed—a relationship with an existing *order* of which *iustum est ut omnia sint ordinatissima* [it is right that all things be perfectly ordered] (St. Augustine, *De libero arbitrio*, 1, 6, 15).

It is an order linked with the very universe of being and intrinsic to that universe of being. If I discover that this relationship is contrary to it—that is, conscience perceives that this action is contrary to that order, that this action destroys that order and upsets it—*this* action, precisely because of its deformation, must be avoided. Moral conscience knows this order of being in that it is respected or negated by the action I am about to perform. Therefore, the judgment of the conscience—and it deserves a great deal of attention—is the convergence, the meeting point, the synthesis of *knowledge about the intrinsic order of being* with *knowledge about the action* I am about to perform. This order intrinsic to being is none other than the order of God's creative wisdom with and in which everything created has been created.

But how can man know this order, this "ontological rectitude"? This human capability is precisely what is called *human reason.* It is thus what makes man participate in the wisdom of God: the seal stamped on man—and only on man—by God's creative hand. Through reason man knows the order that represents the beauty and goodness of being. It is in the light of this knowledge that conscience can discover whether the action which a person is about to perform is found in this order, in this beauty and goodness. To say that this order is created or made up by human reason and not merely discovered by it amounts simply to denying a fact to which our experience continuously testifies. When we discover this beauty with our reason, this order and its unchangeable requirements, *non examinator corrigit, sed tantum laetatur inventor* [it does not judge (them) as an arbiter but it enjoys them as a discoverer], as Saint Augustine profoundly wrote (*De libero arbitrio*, 2, 12, 34). I will now try to explain this most important point.

Let us begin with an observation. On what man has produced, we make a judgment (*examinatores corrigimus*, Saint Augustine would say). Looking at a building, we say: "It could or should have been built better." Or of a book: "It's not well written. It could or should have been written better." And so on.

But none of us, when we discover that justice deserves being honored, would say: "It could or should have been different. It would have been better if justice had not merited being honored." Very simply when we see the dignity of justice, we see a truth that does not depend on us, about which we cannot make a judgment. We see instead that we depend on it and are judged by it, and we delight in that discovery (*laetatur inventor*).

Now let us return to our topic to conclude it. Human reason partakes of the light of God's creative wisdom, which governs the entire universe of being. Through this participation man discovers an intrinsic order of being which must be recognized and venerated. In the light of this discovery, man is in a position to judge whether an action he is about to perform is within this order (= good) or negates it (= evil). This judgment is precisely moral conscience. I cannot find any better synthesis or conclusion than these words by Newman:

> The Supreme Being . . . has the attributes of justice, truth, wisdom, sanctity, benevolence, and mercy, as eternal characteristics in his nature, the very Law of his being, identical with himself; and next, when he became Creator, he implanted this Law, which is himself, in the intelligence of all his rational creatures. The Divine Law, then, is the rule of ethical truth, the standard of right and wrong, a sovereign, irreversible, absolute authority in the presence of men and Angels. . . . This Law, as apprehended in the minds of

individual men, is called "conscience" (*Letter to the Duke of Norfolk*, in *Difficulties of Anglicans*, II, pp. 246–47).

1.2 Moral conscience and the Church's Magisterium

It is not necessary for me to recall the Catholic doctrine concerning the Church's Magisterium. I presuppose it to be well known.

From what we have said previously it immediately follows that the supreme good for conscience is that the person know the truth about what is right and wrong; that he see that intrinsic order of being, intuit the beauty of righteousness, and know the unchangeable requirements of that order (= moral norms). Without this knowledge, conscience is lacking that light that enables it to see the good or the evil of the act to be performed. This knowledge is for conscience what light is for the eyes. Without light the eye simply cannot see. How can I judge a page of music if I have no musical sense? How can I judge an action from a moral point of view if I do not know the norms on which to base a judgment? On the other hand, that conscience judge in the light of truth is the most necessary thing—indeed, the only absolutely necessary thing for man. On this depends whether he is in truth or in error and his *eternal* destiny.

Let us keep all this in mind and, at the same time, what man's *real* situation is in this matter: he is exposed to error, uncertainty, and the difficulty of discovering the truth about what is right and wrong. From this we can already presume that, in his Providence, God wanted to remedy this situation in order not to leave man in such great spiritual difficulty.

The moral Magisterium of the Church is precisely the gift of Providence to man. It teaches the unchangeable requirements of the moral order so that, in its light, the judgment of conscience can be true. Thus to speak of a conflict between conscience and Magisterium is the same as speaking of a conflict between the eye and the light. The eye does not find in the light anything that hinders it from seeing; rather, the light is the medium through which the eye can see. In this context we can find the ultimate roots of a situation that frequently occurs today.

If it is believed that conscience represents moral truth or, in the final analysis, that it is not called to accept a truth or to make its own and interiorize more and more deeply a truth which it did not create, then a potential competitor of conscience, its adversary, can be seen in the Magisterium. The same thing can actually happen if one is not convinced that the Magisterium possesses that *charisma certum veritatis* [secure gift of truth] which Christ wanted for it.

In this context we can and must rigorously clarify the concept of "rights of conscience".

First of all, the way of conceiving the relationship between conscience and political authority cannot be transferred to the relationship between conscience and Magisterium. The scope of the former extends *only as far as* the requirements of the "common good": the end of the political society. The attainment of this end, which political authority seeks through the promulgation of laws, includes no more than the performance of certain *external* actions and the omission of others. The end of the political community is in fact a *temporal* one. It obviously does not propose man's eternal salvation. Thus the human person has a higher value than the political community as such. The latter only has an instrumental value with regard to the human person: it exists *for* the human person. Thus with regard to the political community, or more precisely to political authority, the human person is an intangible value. And if the authority were not to respect that intangibility, it would perform a morally illicit act and the person would not only have the right but the duty to refuse to obey (= conscientious objection in the case, for example, of the law legitimizing abortion).

The situation of the person in the Church is profoundly different. It should never be forgotten, not even for an instant, that the Church is that event that originates in Christ's redemptive act, the event of man's eternal salvation. The Church has only one reason for being: to lead man to eternal communion with God. The Church, in its basic mystery, is not the work of man: it is the new Jerusalem that *came down from heaven.* Its root is the faith that assents to God's revelation. It is built through consent to the love of Christ, who gives himself on the Cross, the gift which is always present through the Eucharist. The Magisterium is one of the means created by Christ himself in order for the Church to remain faithful to her spouse: that she not be adulterous by giving herself to others. Remaining in the truth of Christ is the first condition for the very *existence* of the Church. In order thus to remain, the Magisterium exists. And we have now reached the *heart* of our problem: the conflict—to use again the words of Newman—between the "dogmatic principle" and the "liberal principle". The "liberal principle" can be described in this way:

> That truth and falsehood in religion are but matter of opinion; that one doctrine is as good as another; that the governor of the world does not intend that we should gain the truth; that there is no truth; that we are not more acceptable to God by believing this than by believing that; that no one is answerable for his opinions; that they are a matter of necessity or accident; that it is enough if we sincerely hold what we profess; that our merit lies in seeking not in possessing; that it is a duty to follow what seems to us

true, without a fear lest it should not be true; . . . that we may take up and lay down opinions at pleasure; . . . that we may safely trust to our selves in matters of faith and need no other guide (*Essay on the Development of Christian Doctrine*, Westminster 1968, pp. 357-58).

The "dogmatic principle" can be described as follows:

That there is a truth then; that there is one truth; that religious error is in itself of an immoral nature; that its maintainers, unless unvoluntarily such, are guilty in maintaining it; that it is to be dreaded; that the search for truth is not the gratification of curiosity; that its attainment has nothing of the excitement of a discovery; that the mind is below truth, not above it, and is bound not to descant upon it but to venerate it; that truth and falsehood are set before us for the trial of our hearts; . . . that before all things it is necessary to hold the Catholic faith; that he that would be saved must thus think, and not otherwise (*Essay on the Development of Christian Doctrine*, p. 357).

These two principles describe exactly the two attitudes with which we can ultimately place ourselves in the Church. The first principle is the antiecclesial one par excellence since it simply denies that which *makes* the Church *be*: obedient acceptance of *revealed truth*.

Within the context of the liberal principle one can say that in the Church, as in states, there must be religious freedom. One speaks of "rights of conscience" against the Magisterium since, coherently, the liberal principle logically leads to denying that a truth exists which is imposed on conscience or to holding that the existence or nonexistence of the truth is a matter of secondary importance for man's salvation or to believing it impossible that a Magisterium exists which possesses *as such* a *real authority of its own*. Therefore, any intervention by the Magisterium in the field of moral truth will either be judged as undue interference in the area of conscience or be seen as one of the many voices to which conscience does not owe real obedience.

Within the context of the dogmatic principle, one can speak of "rights of conscience" which are not *against* the Magisterium but precisely the opposite. The faithful has the right that the Magisterium teach him moral truth. Conscience has a right *to* the Magisterium. In this sense, Saint Augustine wrote that to be a Christian is a dignity, to be a pastor is a service (cf., for example, *Disc.*, 1-2; *CCL*, 41, pp. 529-30).

2. MORAL CONSCIENCE, MAGISTERIUM OF THE CHURCH, RESPONSIBLE PROCREATION

In the light of what we have said up to now, we can now go into our specific topic. We will carry out our reflection on the basis of the catecheses which the Holy Father dedicated to the Encyclical *Humanae Vitae* in the Wednesday audiences. There are sixteen catecheses, which began on July 7, 1984, and ended on November 28, 1984.

I would like to note immediately that I do not intend to present their content but simply to reread them in the context of the theme given to me.

2.1 The problem

It must immediately be noted that the problem we are dealing with is not explicitly raised in these catecheses. However, there are two explicit statements touching on the subject of conscience, or rather—if we take what is quoted into consideration as well—there are four (cf. *The Teaching of John Paul II*, VII, no. 2-1984, pp. 87, 101; quotes: *GS*, no. 50, p. 145). The two quotations contain a statement of great importance: the moral norm taught by *Humanae Vitae* is based on the intimate nature of the conjugal act, of the very person of the spouses; and, through the rereading in the truth of that intimate nature, it must be transferred to the *conscience* of the spouses.

The statement must be carefully analyzed. As we know, the main nucleus of the teaching of *Humanae Vitae* is this: the conjugal act bears within itself two meanings—the unitive and the procreative—and the two are inseparably connected.

By making use of the term *significance*, Paul VI expresses a correlation between the conjugal act *which signifies* and a subject to which *the significance*, the "significant message", is made. In order to understand better, we can recall the analogy of a communication based on words between two persons. There is one person who speaks and communicates a message and the other person who listens and grasps the significance of the words spoken. Similarly the conjugal act has *in itself* two meanings which are inseparably connected. These two meanings and their inseparable connection must be understood, "read in their truth". Through this "reading in truth", the truth of the conjugal act enters into the spouses' conscience.

According to classical metaphysics of human knowledge, the truth, speaking correctly and formally, consists of the judgment of our reason; it is a property of the judgment of our reason (in technical terms, this is logical truth). But when are our judgments true? When the way in which our thought is formulated about the matter corresponds to the way in which the matter exists. "Truth", says Saint Thomas, "is the conformity of the mind with being in that [the mind] states about being what it is and not what it is not" (*CG*, I, p. 59). Thus the basis of the truth (logic) of our judgments is reality itself in that it is knowable in itself. Hence a truth exists in things themselves which, when known, renders our judgments true. This "truth about things" is called *ontological truth* (which precedes and gives foundation to logical truth).

After this brief digression, let us return to our subject. In one of his catecheses, the Holy Father states: "Meaning arises in the conscience with the rereading of the truth (ontological) of the object. Through this rereading the truth (ontological) enters, so to speak, into the cognitive dimension: subjective and psychological" (no. 1, p. 101). This paragraph is very important. Let us try briefly to examine it.

The conjugal act possesses a truth of its own (ontological). When this truth is known, the truth about the conjugal act enters into the conscience, and the subject knows *really* what the conjugal act is. That is, he sees the two basic meanings and their inseparable connection. Therefore, the intimate structure of the conjugal act (about which *Humanae Vitae* speaks) is the basis, the foundation, for discovering those two meanings and their inseparable connection. This discovery is made by conscience, which then transfers those two meanings into one's personal subjectivity. The person accepts them, reads about them, and interiorizes them so that they become the norm of his behavior. But note well: the existence of these two meanings in the conjugal act and their inseparable connection are not caused by the fact that conscience discovers them: they exist prior to conscience. Saint Augustine writes: "Truth, while remaining unto itself, does not grow when it is manifested more greatly to us, nor does it diminish when manifested less to us, but it remains integral and always the same. It fills with light those who turn to it and punishes with blindness those who shun it" (*De libero arbitrio*, 2, 12, 34). It is not the eye that turns on the light nor does the light shine more because more eyes are enlightened by it. What becomes more or less luminous is the eye and not the light. If, when thirsty, you drink more water, the fountain will not make more water flow. And, in this way, the truth about the conjugal act does not depend on awareness about it. Thus there is no sense in talking about a "graduality of the moral law".

It must be noted, however, that it is not a truth outside of man. It is rather, as the catecheses emphasize repeatedly, the very truth (ontological) of the human person. Thus the conscience cannot dispense with knowing about it. By not knowing the truth, man will not act *in truth*; he will not do what is true and will lose his freedom. He will create an existence in error—a nonexistence.

The reason then for *Humanae Vitae* and the catecheses on human love is to enlighten men and women about the truth of their conjugal love, about the truth of their being human persons. It is a concrete case of the implementation of that profound relationship between moral conscience and Magisterium which we discussed at length in the first part of this report.

2.2 Our task

What is our task then? In the first place to communicate wholly this Magisterium of the Church. But we must reflect on this communication, at least briefly.

First, we must be convinced and aware that the truth communicated is not "something extraneous to man". It is not an ideal: it is *the truth* about man. Thus it is a truth which each man bears inscribed in his heart. The Church does not teach an ideal: she teaches the truth *about man*. Christian pedagogy is a pedagogy of the "inner teacher" and not a "product of consensus". The Christian pedagogue guides man to discovering in himself the truth of which he is made.

Second, we must remember the particularly difficult situation in which man, given his sinful condition, finds himself in seeking moral truth. An environment and a life of chastity help decisively in perceiving the ethical value of the conjugal act.

Conclusion

"This is our freedom: to be subject to the truth, . . . that very truth which is also man in dialogue with other men, dictated to those who believe in him: if you keep my words, you will be my disciples. You will know the truth and the truth will make you free" (*De libero arbitrio*, 2, 13, 37).

The Magisterium of the Church exists so that spouses, by listening through it to Christ's words, may know the truth about their conjugal love: the truth about their being spouses. May this truth penetrate their moral conscience and their decisions since joy is basically possessing the truth.

UNION AND PROCREATION IN MARRIAGE AND CONJUGAL LIFE

MSGR. FRANCISCO GIL HELLÍN

Defects of the conjugal institution

When the Council Fathers examined the text of the chapter in *Gaudium et Spes* dedicated to marriage, after expressing the esteem and regard which this institution enjoys today in society, they noted the shortcomings and defects also present in our times which negatively affect the conjugal community. Among these, some are external to the institution but can cause serious disturbances, as, for instance, certain economic, sociopsychological, and civil conditions. Other factors affect it intrinsically and even directly deform the very institution of marriage or destroy its life—that is, conjugal love.

Among the factors inimical to the conjugal institution, polygamy, the plague of divorce, and so-called free love can be named because they deny and reject one of the basic characteristics of marriage—its unity and indissolubility—or the institution itself. But if these enemies are great and serious ones for marriage, we cannot disregard the malice of others which, while not directly attacking the institution, contribute effectively to its destruction by voiding its content and meaning. About this the Council adds: "Conjugal love is frequently profaned by egoism, hedonism, and illicit practices against procreation" (*GS*, no. 47).

How such practices, which profane conjugal love, can contribute to deforming the institution of marriage is not easy to perceive at first glance. If one considers that marriage is the institution for conjugal love, it can be more clearly seen that everything either favors or detracts from the spouses' love, reaffirms or negates in practice the *truth* about this institution. It is not by chance that those who wish to eliminate the institution as such and proclaim free love as an ideal for future society encourage and foster all sorts of contraception and abortion. They defend them as rights of the person, when they are really only expressions of the most base selfishness and hedonism, which is unchecked even with regard to the rights of an already-conceived human being. If we wish to destroy the institution of marriage, let us promote—they would say—the passions that touch on the properties of that institution.

In the same way, it is not by chance that the Church's Magisterium and concretely the Pope's catechesis on marriage and the doctrine of the Encyclical *Humanae Vitae* insist upon marriage. Its teaching is of outstanding value not only as a presentation of the moral norms of conjugal life. The entire vision of marriage is defended in it because the rectitude of conjugal life is required and determined by the essence of marriage. "The reflections", says the Pope in the first of his catecheses, "which have been made until now about human love on the divine level would remain somehow incomplete if we did not see the direct application in the framework of conjugal and family morality. . . . Let us go back and reread that meaningful document [*Humanae Vitae*] in the light of the results we have reached by examining the original divine plan and Christ's words which refer to it."

Of course, orthodoxy is one thing and orthodox practice is another. Thus practical incoherence in conjugal life may follow a clear understanding and acceptance of the essence of marriage, without necessarily bringing about doctrinal change. But this is possible if an effort is made at coherence, conversion, recognition of one's own weakness and sinfulness, and a desire to docilely accept grace. If, on the other hand, this attitude is lacking—that is, the effort to adjust one's life to the doctrine—it is to be expected that one's own life will be taken as the reference point for modifying the doctrine.

Thus the Pope's catecheses are important not only in protecting men of goodwill, and especially Christians, against practical disorientation in their married life, but also, at the same time and primarily, in enlightening minds to the right order of things desired by God, thereby avoiding diminished understanding, which would lead to the loss of some basic values for human life. It is not difficult to imagine some milieus or countries that accept, without the least difficulty, some practices against the moral rectitude of married life and that have already begun legalizing and justifying conjugal unions which are in opposition to the very nature of the diversity of the sexes.

Indispensable and complementary requirements

The Holy Father focuses his first catechesis on *Humanae Vitae* on a part of the Encyclical which has a special meaning for understanding the moral doctrine contained in the document. "The Church teaches that each and every marriage act must remain open to the transmission of life" (*HV*, no. 11). There are those who believe that this doctrine, which already appeared in Pius XI's Encyclical *Casti Connubii*, had been modified by Vatican II. A clear distinction must be made between what some experts and Council Fathers intended and what was actually affirmed and expressed in the documents of the ecumenical assembly. Paul VI certainly kept to himself his opinion about contraceptive pills, and the council document does not concretely touch on these. But when it deals with conjugal life, the judgment it gives does set up the boundaries of moral rectitude with regard to the spouses' intimate life. The moral nature of the spouses' intimate life—says the Council—is determined by those objective criteria which respect the full meaning of self-giving and human procreation in the context of true love. The two complementary and indispensable requirements which are specific to the *goodness* of intimate married life are thus mutual conjugal giving and the openness of this giving to procreation. This requirement is neither procreation as a sole and absolute value, nor is it conjugal giving closed to life. It is rather procreation as the fruit of the spouses' mutual giving or, what is the same, a mutual giving that is in itself open to life.

Thus the content of the statement in *Humanae Vitae* that "each and every marriage act must remain open to the transmission of life" is not new. Besides affirming the principle of conjugal morality, Paul VI's Encyclical presents the inseparable connection that exists between the two meanings of the conjugal act: that it be both and necessarily one of union and one of procreation. "That teaching, often set forth by the Magisterium"—as Paul VI says in *Humanae Vitae* and John Paul II recalls in his catechesis—"is based on the inseparable connection, established by God, which man on his initiative may not break, between the unitive significance and the procreative significance, both of which are inherent to the marriage act."

Motivations

The reason for this inseparable union of the two meanings of the conjugal union as requirements of its morality—Paul VI continues—arises from the very nature of the conjugal act, which "because of its fundamental structure, while it unites husband and wife in the closest intimacy, also brings into operation laws written into the actual nature of man and of woman for the generation of new life" (*HV*, no. 12). And, as John Paul II continues in his analysis: "The passage from the sentence expressing the moral norm to the sentence which explains and justifies it is especially significant. The Encyclical leads one to seek the foundation for the norm, which determines the morality of the actions of the man and the woman in the marriage act, in the nature of this very act, and, more deeply still, in the nature of the subjects themselves who are performing the act" (catechesis of July 11, 1984, no. 5).

These two meanings—the unitive and procreative—make up the subjective and psychological dimension of the truth contained in the very reality of the conjugal union. Thus the ontological dimension grasped by human understanding according to truth is cognitively expressed as the procreative and unitive aspects of conjugal life. As John Paul II says in his catechesis of July 18, 1984: "The 'significance' becomes known with the *rereading of the* (ontological) *truth of the object.* Through this rereading, the (ontological) truth enters, so to speak, into the cognitive dimension: subjective and psychological" (no. 1).

Hence these are not aspects of meaning which the thinking subject raises but aspects which he finds in the reality contained in the very essence of conjugal communion. To state it in another way, it is the conjugal act itself which, "because of its fundamental structure, while it unites husband and wife in the closest intimacy, also brings into operation laws written into the actual nature of man and of woman for the generation of new life". These "laws" are the ontological basis of the unitive and procreative meaning of conjugal life and thereby of its moral laws. The Encyclical *Humanae Vitae* contains the moral norm and its reason, or at least an indication of what represents the reason for that norm. Furthermore, because in the norm the moral value is expressed in a binding way, it follows that actions which conform to the norm are morally right, while those actions which are contrary to it are intrinsically illicit (catechesis, July 18, 1984).

Thus the Church's Magisterium, in Vatican Council II's *Gaudium et Spes*, and specifically in Paul VI's Encyclical *Humanae Vitae* and in John Paul II's Apostolic Exhortation *Familiaris Consortio*, as well as in the catechesis on marriage, has made very clear the absolute inseparability of the unitive and procreative aspects, which are both required for the moral rectitude of conjugal life. Any act of contraception, even if motivated by the intent of cultivating a greater union between spouses, by positively excluding openness to a possible transmission of life, destroys the goodness of the conjugal act.

What then is the ultimate nature of the conjugal act which renders absolutely inseparable the unitive and procreative aspects on a moral level? Why is it a *sole* moral value that implies both—and necessarily—the total giving of the person and openness to life which could potentially start?

The *moral* value of the conjugal union

All experts on conjugal morality admit the dual meaning of the conjugal act. Not all, however, accept that the moral value of the marriage union depends on the inseparable presence of these two aspects—unitive and procreative. In the case of falling in love, for example, so many qualities can have an influence: beauty, amiability, culture, talent, social position. But while they are elements which in themselves are positive and contribute to increasing the overall worth of the loved one, none of these qualities is indispensable in obtaining the assent of the loved one. The absence of some of these values does not necessarily annul his goodness, even if it may lessen it.

Now, when it is a question of the moral value of the conjugal act, the two aspects are necessary and inseparable. What is the reason? Why aren't those two aspects or meanings like two values that amount to the total value?

Why does not each of these two values contribute on its own to enriching the goodness of married life? They could then be cultivated separately from one another, especially when some reason, at least a serious one, made their development together difficult. Examining *why* they are not two separate values but *two necessary aspects of one value* helps in understanding the Church's doctrine better. If they are two necessary aspects of one single moral value, the absence of the unitive or procreative aspect destroys the moral goodness of the conjugal act. But what concretely is the reason for the natural goodness of the conjugal act and therefore of the intrinsic evil of excluding one of these two essential aspects?

We are now looking at the main nucleus of this exposé. Because the Church's Magisterium has affirmed the doctrine of the required openness to life of each and every conjugal act as an intrinsic requirement of its moral goodness, and this truth is founded, on the other hand, on the very intimate structure of the conjugal act, as Vatican Council, *Humanae*

Vitae, and the Pope's catechesis affirm, let us now try to discover the reason which necessarily binds these two aspects of the conjugal act inseparably in such a way that they are not really two values in themselves but two aspects of the same value: human procreation and human conjugality. Each of these two expressions, even though each directly refers to one of the aspects, also implies the other: in order for human procreation to be a moral value, it must be a fruit of nuptial self-giving, while nuptial giving, in order to be such, must not exclude the potential life it could initiate.

Truth and falsehood in marriage

The title of this presentation is: "Union and Procreation in Marriage and Conjugal Life". According to what we have said previously—and as Msgr. Caffarra has pointed out—the doctrine of the Church's Magisterium affirms the unitive and procreative aspects as essential characteristics of the goodness of conjugal life. We would like to add that these two aspects are intrinsic to the very *essence of marriage*; that is, a natural marriage is precisely the total mutual giving of man and woman in openness to life. Furthermore, we would like to see the relationship between these two professed aspects of marriage and the conjugal act because they are professed as essential and inseparable for both marriage and the conjugal act. In both—marriage and the conjugal act—because they make up its essence, they define its goodness—that is, the existence of marriage and the moral rectitude of the conjugal act.

The reason is found, in my opinion, in the fact that the conjugal act of the spouses *reflects* the goodness of the essence of marriage. Thus, conjugal union is morally licit—that is, it is a value of the spouses—when it is a coherent expression of married life and when it is a manifestation of the truth about what marriage *is*. If it is not, that act in the life of the spouses is a *falsehood* and negates in practice the truth contained in the essence of marriage, whose light should shine through.

Well then, what is the truth about marriage? Any analysis of the essence of marriage leads to detecting two basic elements. These define what marriage is: mutual conjugal self-giving, openness to life. These two aspects are precisely what Saint Augustine called *bonum fidei* and *bonum prolis*. Both inseparably united represent the *goods* of marriage on which it depends absolutely. The first—mutual self-giving in indivisible unity—must be positively willed by those contracting marriage. The second, in turn—openness to the transmission of human life—requires that it not be positively excluded. The reason for the sufficiency of this noncontrary intention is found in the intrinsic natural orientation of mutual self-giving to the transmission of life. In the absence of an active, contrary intention, the free decision that characterizes mutual self-giving of the spouses also affects, at least implicitly, its natural end: the procreation of children.

This entire statement concerns the *natural* goodness of marriage. The mutual self-giving of the spouses and their openness to life are the two aspects which make up the intrinsic goodness of natural marriage and which are absolutely inseparable. Even if one can speak of *bonum fidei* and *bonum prolis* separately, there cannot be a genuinely good marriage that excludes one of these. Nor does one of these two values in the absence of the other possess real moral value. In fact, one cannot speak of the *moral* value of procreation as openness to life in a union of fornication, much less in an adulterous one. But neither can a moral *value* be expressed by mutual self-giving which positively excludes openness to procreation. The reason is that in none of these cases does true marriage exist. The appearance of marriage in the first case gives rise to actions or states which are intrinsically illicit because they lack mutual self-giving either because the spouses do not want it or are incapable of it. No one can give what does not belong to him. In the same way, in the second case, there is the positive rejection of the right to the transmission of life. Any pretext at mutual self-giving is ineffectual in giving a moral basis to conjugal life. The openness to life and the desire for mutual self-giving considered exclusively do not attenuate or lessen in any way the intrinsic evil of the preceding cases.

If this analysis concerning the intrinsic goodness of marriage is now applied to the specific act of conjugal union, the reason for the inseparable unity of the unitive and the procreative aspects of the conjugal act will appear more clearly. It flows as a logical consequence that the voluntary exclusion of these aspects gives rise not just to diminishing its goodness but to the actual destruction of the moral value which every natural conjugal act contains. This is the reason for the intrinsic evil both of all extramarital unions and of all contraceptive actions.

The intimate union of spouses, as a specific act of marriage, reflects in itself the nature of what marriage is. Thus the conjugal act must be the mutual, total self-giving of body and spirit, open to the transmission of life. In the nature of the conjugal act there are two aspects, unitive and procreative, which define its morality. When both exist, the act is intrinsically good; on the contrary, when one or the other is lacking by positive human will, the act will become intrinsically evil.

The intention of the spouses

Although both aspects belong inseparably to the intrinsic goodness of the conjugal act, it is not necessary that both must be equal in the spouses' intention. Mutual giving must be positively desired by each one, but their orientation toward or openness to offspring does not require that this be directly intended in every conjugal act, only that it not be excluded. Given the natural and intrinsic orientation of the conjugal union to new life, the absence of a positively contrary intention is the sufficient requisite for openness to life, which, together with real mutual self-giving, constitutes the moral value of the conjugal act.

This natural goodness of the spouses' intimate act is destroyed by the exclusion of the unitive or the procreative aspect or of both at the same time. The spouses' act is certainly intrinsically illicit if, while remaining open to life, it is not an expression of mutual self-giving to one another, as in the case of adultery of spirit, in which the husband or wife is the concrete factor in self-giving, but the desire is for another person. Such an act is not the expression of the *truth* and thus of the goodness of marriage because it is not a reflection of personal and mutual conjugal self-giving, even if one's spouse were to accept the other's adulterous thoughts. This lack of mutual and personal self-giving, even if it were intended better to guarantee offspring, is also the reason for the intrinsic evil of test-tube fertilization, even in the case where the vital elements come from the spouses and are later implanted in the wife. The act which gave rise to such life was not one of the spouses' mutual, personal self-giving.

In the same way, the conjugal act is intrinsically evil when it intends to reflect the mutual self-giving characteristic of the essence of marriage while positively excluding fecundity. The reason is that not only does it not reflect the goodness of the mutual self-giving belonging to marriage, despite the spouses' possible goodwill, but, because, in practice, it also denies the truth about that self-giving which, because it is conjugal, implies its openness to life. Contraception is not intrinsically evil only because it positively excludes an essential aspect of conjugal life but also because it is, in fact, opposed to the other element of mutual self-giving which at times it claims to serve.

The case is different, as follows from all that has been said previously, when sexual activity takes place during the naturally infertile periods, when serious reasons exist, as the Magisterium constantly recalls. Otherwise, such behavior by spouses would not be far from the error of selfishness. The difference between the use of infertile periods and any type of contraception is clear. Supposing that in both cases the unitive aspect of the conjugal act were respected, the moral difference depends on the different attitude toward the procreative aspect. Although through the use of infertile periods this aspect, which is not sought, is respected in its roots, in contraception, it is avoided and negated. It is one thing not to want it and another positively to exclude it. The difference lies between what one does not directly intend and what is positively excluded, or, rather, between a negative intention and a contrary one.

In applying this same difference to the essence of marriage, the exemplary cause of the morality of the conjugal act, those who contract marriage without the desire to have children, if they do not exclude them, have contracted a valid marriage. Those, on the contrary, who enter into marriage with a positive intention contrary to procreation have certainly not contracted marriage, even if in fact they later accept having children.

The evil of contraception, where a positive intention exists contrary to the procreative aspect of the conjugal act, is one thing. Quite another is the morality of using infertile periods, where only a negative intention exists regarding the same procreative aspect of the marriage union. That positive contrary intention, in addition to the desired unfruitfulness of the conjugal act, which is also present in the negative intention, further implies an action which is sufficient cause in itself of the desired unfruitfulness.

Conclusion

The desire to apply to intimate marital life the achievements of dominion over the forces of nature by separating the two natural meanings of the conjugal act—even if to protect or develop one of them—is not something that pertains exclusively to the biological or psychological plane. This implies a fundamental dimension of the human being because both aspects are projected in the conjugal act as essential to the essence of marriage, which is the first and principal expression of man as a social being.

HUMAN DIFFICULTIES AND CLARIFICATIONS OF THE CHURCH'S MAGISTERIUM ON CONJUGAL LIFE

WLADYSLAW BERNARD SKRZYDLEWSKI, O.P.

Because the title of this report is so broadly stated, it is necessary to define it. It does not deal with all the possible problems linked to conjugal life but to those relating to conjugal life in a stricter sense: the spouses' sexual life. Nevertheless, at the beginning we must take a glance at conjugal life in general in order to see what moral consequences arise from it for conjugal life in the stricter sense.

I. Conjugal life from a theological perspective

What is conjugal life from a theological viewpoint? Human life is the way to salvation. What a psychologist calls "life" is "the way to salvation" for a theologian. Conjugal life is the way to salvation for a couple. When a man and a woman decide to marry, they decide to walk together in their life in common, thus to make their way to salvation together. It is a completely new way. Until the day of their marriage, they were individually responsible for their salvation, each one only for his or her salvation. From the moment they marry, they are responsible for their salvation before God together, in common. From that time they are integrated into Christ's great sacrament together as in a community of salvation. They can no longer walk toward their salvation singly but must walk together. And they are responsible for leading their entire family to salvation, this new community of salvation, which is a living and dynamic community: not only a community or a structure but a reality of life, a community of members of their family with the living God. For this reason marriage is a sacrament of salvation, and the spouses' life, even their sexual life, has a sacramental value providing that it is not distorted.

II. The tasks and meaning of conjugal life

What are the special tasks which spouses must perform in walking toward their salvation together? Once they were called "the ends of marriage". The word *ends* was not good from a methodological point of view. Certain ends can be achieved and others sought, while the goals of marriage are always the same during the entire life of the spouses. For that reason, today one speaks about "the tasks of the family" and not only of marriage because the whole family takes part in the achievement of these tasks: the children's education and help to the spouses along their path to salvation.

In speaking of the spouses' sexual life, it must be noted that this represents the core of the realization of their tasks because the spouses' sexual life has a unitive meaning in their personal communion and a procreative meaning in their family vocation. These two tasks cannot be carried out fully except in love, and precisely in the spouses' sexual union does love find the height of its expression. In love, one meaning stimulates the other: the spouses' love union makes the procreation of children joyful and their education effective. Realizing the procreative meaning in love makes the spouses' personal union more compact through the presence of children, who represent the common task of the spouses. This is the truth of God the Creator's design, the design of love. It is why one cannot eliminate either of the two meanings in the act that constitutes the spouses' sexual life. Otherwise, the conjugal act would be deprived of truth and true love, and would become falsified and deviate into selfishness. The presence of these two basic meanings of the conjugal act is important and necessary for the spouses' happiness, for their personal and mutual growth, and for the development of humanity. These are the requirements of human realization of conjugal, sexual life.

III. The "hope" for contraception and the "disappointment" of the Encyclical *Humanae Vitae*

The difficulties connected with realizing the conjugal tasks are perhaps as old as mankind itself. We know today that contraception and some methods of natural planning of conceptions were not invented in modern times. But the technical inventions of the fifties and sixties of our age in the area of contraception raised great hopes which were further stimulated by the fear of the world population explosion. People wanted to use the pill and the IUD, while believing Catholics waited for the assent of the Church's Magisterium.

When, on the contrary, in his 1968 Encyclical *Humanae Vitae* Paul VI condemned all contraception and recommended only natural family planning, it provoked a storm of indignation. The French episcopacy accepted contraception as a necessary choice between two evils, even though Paul VI expressly rejected this possibility in the Encyclical because there is no choice between two evils when there is a third positive solution: natural planning. The German episcopacy in its declaration *Königsteiner Erklärung* and the Austrian episcopacy in the declaration *Maria Trost Erklärung* left the choice between contraception and natural planning to the individual conscience as if the whole world were expert in biology, medicine, and morality. Theologians made efforts to deny the binding nature of the Encyclical and to find arguments contrary to its solutions. They asked for contraception to be approved according to two criteria: the maximum effectiveness and minimum harm of the means and methods used.

A silence of contempt surrounded Paul VI for ten years following the publication of the Encyclical *Humanae Vitae*. In family counseling centers in the West, even in Catholic centers, almost only contraceptive methods were taught. Permissive theologians were so sure of their positive opinion about contraception that they did not follow the results of medical research and did not learn of the changes which had taken place.

IV. A medical judgment of contraception

Ten years after the publication of the Encyclical *Humanae Vitae*, it was already known that the effectiveness of contraceptive methods was no greater than that of natural planning methods based on observation of ovulation symptoms. It was also known, at least among experts, that all contraceptive methods were seriously harmful.

Perhaps the oldest contraceptive method, *coitus interruptus*, leads to serious neuroses in both spouses. Less known but also certain is the observation that all mechanical contraceptive means, male and female, cause inflammation in the woman, creating, over a long period, serious conditions or the need for surgery. Hormonal disturbances, sterility, and other consequences of organic degeneration caused by contraceptive pills or injections are well known. Finally, the morning-after pills and all types of IUDs, considered as the fourth and last type of contraceptive means, are really abortive means which kill the child after conception, generally after a few days of life.

Some theologians, such as Josef Fuchs and Bernard Häring, wanted to salvage the IUD by stating that the human embryo does not become a human being until after a certain time. This thesis, however, has not found support from biology and medicine. The result is that every so-called contraceptive method is seen to be either abortive or so harmful that in it there is the basis of a serious sin.

A few words should be added concerning the psychological harmfulness of contraception. First, there is the negative influence of contraception on family life due to the nervousness and tension between spouses as shown by the research of P. Chauchard, W. Póltawska, and others. Second, there is the social effect of psychological demobilization resulting from the atrophy of the spirit to sacrifice—which brings about a demographic catastrophe in developed countries, and a social catastrophe because of a spirit of consumerism in developing countries.

I have presented here a criticism of contraception from the point of view of the empirical sciences. Arguments against contraception are not lacking from the ethical and theological viewpoints.

V. A moral judgment of contraception

We have already seen why Paul VI stated in the Encyclical *Humanae Vitae* that the two meanings of conjugal life cannot be separated—the procreative from the unitive—since both constitute conjugal love and make up the reason for the existence of the conjugal community. They are inseparable not only in the overall life of the couple but also in each act of conjugal sexual life because human morality is the morality of human actions. They are either meritorious or sinful. They are acts for which human persons or couples will have to account before God as judge. That is why Paul VI stated that each marriage act must remain open to life—a statement that shook public opinion but which was well founded.

By deforming the act of the couples' sexual life, all contraception means a distortion of conjugal life. We do not need to recall the discussion concerning the many meanings of the term *nature*. It is a question of its theological and dynamic meaning. It is according to the design of God, the Creator of human nature, that the spouses' common life must fulfill these two tasks: to be saved together and to have children and make them more and more independent in going toward salvation. Separating these two tasks and two meanings of the spouses' sexual life would be to distort it and even dehumanize it because a distorted life is no longer a truly human one.

John Paul II continued Paul VI's thinking in his Apostolic Exhortation *Familiaris Consortio* and developed it in his speech of September 17, 1983, at Castel Gandolfo, in his two final arguments: one is theological, the other anthropological. In the theological argument, John Paul II shows that, by using contraception, the spouses exercise the power to procreate autonomously, although they have received this power from God and are to exercise it only with God, as cooperators. By using contraception, spouses deprive themselves of this power and thus they infringe upon the rights of God the Creator, who is the only one able to decide about human life. They are no longer cooperators with God; they make themselves dominators of human life.

In the second argument, called anthropological, John Paul II recalls that the conjugal act signifies the total and mutual giving of the spouses. When one deprives oneself of one's procreative power, one spouse does not give him- or herself completely to the other in the totality of her femininity or his masculinity. One deprives the other of some part of his or her self, which is an offense against total self-giving and against the totality of love.

In following this thought of John Paul II, it can be said that, by using contraception, one spouse deprives the other of the possibility of becoming a father or mother and of growing by realizing this vocation. It is against conjugal love and against the sacrament of matrimony, which obliges spouses to help one another to reach salvation in addition to reaching the greatest human development.

VI. Objections against natural family planning

Many objections are raised against natural family planning. Some of them have already been dismantled but others are still repeated at times.

1. Those who do not know natural planning well say they cannot use it because the woman has an irregular rhythm of fertility. These people are speaking about the Ogino-Knauss method, the "calendar" method, which is already obsolete. They do not know that modern methods of natural family planning are based on scientific analysis of ovulation symptoms and that they always indicate a precise time.

2. Another objection doubts the effectiveness of natural family planning by citing concrete cases or the percentage of failures. In responding, three types of effectiveness of natural family planning must be distinguished:

a. the effectiveness of the method itself—and this theoretical effectiveness is, in principle, ideal (100 percent);
b. the effectiveness of instruction—and this depends on the instructors' level of preparation and their ability to transmit their knowledge to those receiving instructions;
c. the effectiveness of use—and this depends on the ability of those who are taught to receive instruction and put it into practice correctly.

In reality the natural family planning methods are not difficult. This has been shown in research on the thermal method done by C. Rendu, W. Poltawska, and M. D. Kwapisy, and by the enormous success of the Billings method among illiterate peoples in Africa and Latin America. For this reason, the natural family planning methods are seen to be no less effective than contraceptive pills.

3. By limiting the spouses' sexual life, is natural family planning really natural? Doesn't Saint Thomas Aquinas emphasize the importance of natural inclinations? There is a natural inclination of spouses for sexual relations precisely during the fertile period. Is it not unnatural to transfer these relations to the infertile period when the spouses have less desire?

It must be noted that to act according to natural inclinations does not mean anarchy. A tree is naturally inclined to produce a great number of new branches, but, if allowed to, it will lose its vital forces aimlessly. A good gardener will cut off the poor branches and let only the best ones grow. With human beings, to follow the order set by the Creator does not mean running after every inclination indiscreetly and fulfilling every desire. It is rather realizing one's growth through self-mastery and by concentrating one's psychophysical forces on the most reasonable activities and those which concretize love the best. For spouses it means conjugal love realized in the truth about its meaning.

4. Does not planning spouses' sexual relations eliminate the spontaneity of the conjugal encounter, which is limited to certain specific days? First, one should not confuse spontaneity with disorder or acting out of whim. All human activity must be prudent and responsible and thus planned, especially an activity as important as cooperating with God the Creator in bringing new people into the world. Second, experience shows that if spouses know when they can or should have sexual relations, they become much freer, spontaneous, and joyful than in relations built on whim or based on the use of contraception.

5. Final objection: In order effectively to counteract the population explosion, shouldn't recourse be made to contraception? The experience of developing countries has shown that it is precisely natural family planning that is a truly effective means and that becomes a just demographic policy. On the contrary, contraception has been seen to be a negative factor leading people to a spirit of consumerism, which is an especially dangerous phenomenon in developing countries, where there is need for a spirit of social mobilization and even sacrifice.

VII. The difference between contraception and natural family planning

These final remarks have led us to the point where we can raise the question about the difference between contraception and natural family planning. This is a question rarely posed by representatives of the medical field. Normally in their publications they present natural family planning as one of the contraceptive methods, which is an enormous error. Natural family planning and contraception are not different methods with regard to their final end. They are completely different attitudes and behaviors. Contraception is the flight from and fear of new human life, while natural family planning is a positive choice either for the conception of a new human life or for the realization of conjugal sexual life without such conception. Contraception is closed to life; natural family planning is open to it. Contraception is against human life; natural family planning is for a more reasonable and dignified human life.

From the point of view of the empirical sciences psychology and sociology, attitudes and behavior make up a whole world of human activity. By implementing entirely contrary atitudes and behavior, contraception and natural family planning represent "two different and contrary ways of life".

VIII. The positive value of natural family planning

Because of the misunderstandings about the reality of natural family planning, it has normally been seen and defined negatively only as an alternative to contraception. If someone asks: "Why should we use natural family planning?" one can answer: "Because contraception constitutes a moral evil, and all forms of it are very harmful from a medical point of view." In this way of thinking, the concept of natural family planning comes to be derived from the concept of contraception. From a methodological point of view, this is absurd: a positive phenomenon, natural family planning, is defined by a negative phenomenon—contraception. Good cannot be defined by evil. Natural family planning methods are not used because contraceptive ones are forbidden. It is the opposite case: natural family planning is used because it is the only good and correct way since contraception is a deviation. Using natural family planning represents morally good behavior in itself.

Natural family planning is morally good behavior, first of all, because it represents the realization of the divine plan of creation expressed in the psychophysical structure of man and woman. The woman experiences the rhythm of fertile and infertile periods while her husband is equipped with the intelligence and ability to understand and adapt his behavior to this, thus fulfilling the words of Genesis: "A man is destined to . . . cling to his wife instead, so that two become one flesh" (Gen 2:24). If God wanted the use of contraception, he could have made the woman fertile at all times. He did not do this: he made her fertile only a few days every month, which, on the one hand, guarantees the spouses the possibility of having children. On the other, it also gives them the possibility to conduct their sexual life at a time when conceiving a child would be irresponsible. Because of this sexual make-up, spouses, as Vatican Council II states, can also during infertile periods "through the intimate union of persons express their mutual self-giving by helping one another and striving for and achieving the meaning of their union more and more" (GS, no. 48).

Natural family planning is morally good also because, in achieving a good end, it satisfies the requirements of a morally good means. It does not offend anyone's rights, and it is a responsible activity. As we have already mentioned, all human actions must be responsible and thus prudently planned. The procreation and education of children, being the most important human tasks, should always be kept under control by the spouses: that is, they should be carefully planned. Thus natural family planning is a morally required activity and not one that is permitted.

It should be recalled that Catholic theologians in the fifties considered natural family planning to be permitted only when there were serious reasons for its use. This opinion was reiterated by Pope Pius XII in his famous speech to midwives in 1951.

Wasn't Pius XII right? Yes, he was, because he spoke about limiting conceptions, a negative function. He did not speak about the positive functions of natural family planning. Because having and raising children are basic tasks of the spouses, limiting conceptions, a relatively negative activity, cannot be allowed except for serious reasons.

On the other hand, if one thinks of natural family planning in its positive functions, it represents a morally good and even necessary activity. Having and educating children is the most important activity. It must be carried out wisely and responsibly, thus must be planned. In planning this basic task, spouses must take all the factors at work into consideration. They must guarantee the mother a sufficient amount of time for her physical recuperation between the births of the children; prepare everything necessary for the child's arrival; reflect on the requirements of the common good of the family and of society, as Vatican Council II indicated in the Pastoral Constitution *Gaudium et Spes* (no. 50) and Paul VI in the Encyclical *Humanae Vitae* (no. 10). Natural family planning is not something which is permitted in exceptional circumstances but an attitude and behavior which are necessary and morally obligatory.

Natural family planning has great moral value for still

other reasons because it brings morally good and important effects.

IX. Growth in love—an important effect of natural family planning

Generally, an unexpected but very important effect of natural family planning is the growth of the spouses in love. Even the most spontaneous and authentic love needs to be developed. Love, which is a dynamic virtue, grows through the appropriate acts which express it. Love is shown by the acts which express self-giving by the person who loves. Conjugal love is shown in the acts of giving aimed at making the loved one happy. When a young man loves a young woman, he tries to give her something that will make her happy: sweet words, flowers, etc. This requires a gift and even a little sacrifice. Some time, money, or personal effort must be sacrificed. These acts of sacrifice, which express self-giving to the loved one, make love grow and become more capable of further sacrifices.

Natural family planning is based on observing conjugal continence, called "periodic". It may be a lesser or greater sacrifice. As a result of this sacrifice conjugal love is expressed and grows intensely. It becomes stronger, mutually more attentive, and is expressed with greater tenderness. This gives spouses great spiritual satisfaction, an essential element of their conjugal happiness. Only in such an atmosphere of growing love and happiness can spouses succeed in raising their children well.

X. Other effects of natural family planning

The growth of the spouses' mutual love is an important effect of the continued use of natural family planning, but it is not the only one. There are also other effects. Instead of fear of an unexpected pregnancy, a sense of security begins to grow in the family. Through their cooperation in natural family planning, spouses learn to dominate their sexual instincts and master themselves. They become less nervous and their life is calmer. By being obliged to respect his wife's periods, the husband acquires more respect for her and becomes more attentive. The woman's position in the marriage improves. She is no longer a suffering servant to her husband as dominator. They exchange the expression of their love: embraces, kisses, tenderness. The culture of conjugal and family life is elevated. The atmosphere in the home becomes harmonious. In this united atmosphere, the children's education goes better and is more effective. And, as some women state, because of the change from contraception to natural family planning, their husbands are profoundly changed: from being difficult, brutal, and even evil men, they become attentive, tender, and charming.

Spouses who use natural family planning are aware that it provides the chance to decide better the time to have a new child. A child planned in this way is awaited with love and joy. By dominating the procreative process, spouses can have the desired number of children, while those who use contraception live in fear and rarely have more than one or two children, which is an insufficient number from both a reasonable demographic viewpoint and that of family pedagogy.

While the use of contraception is a serious sin, spouses who use natural family planning properly have no problem in this sense. They know that they remain in the state of grace. Peace of conscience and the possibility of receiving Holy Communion stimulate their religious life and give them great joy. Many of them feel the need to share their knowledge with others. They can satisfy this apostolic spirit by taking part in the work of natural family planning instruction centers or marriage-preparation courses.

XI. Practical conclusions

The great moral value of natural family planning and its important effects, which have been synthetically presented here, show how unreasonable the prejudices are against such planning and in favor of contraception. The consequences must be drawn from this: erroneous opinions must be changed; natural family planning must be introduced into one's conjugal life and efforts made to disseminate such planning methods among the members of one's family, region, and nation.

Naturally, personal effort is not enough. The experiences of Scotland and Poland have proved that only a universal obligation imposed by the national episcopate can produce the desired results. And, of course, sufficient instructors must be prepared and an adequate network of instruction centers set up where only natural family planning methods are taught.

Lastly, the bishops must be encouraged to impose the obligation on all those who are to be married in the Church to participate in marriage-preparation courses and to receive detailed instruction on natural family planning.

It is illusory to think that contraception can be allowed and, at the same time, that there will be a high level of sexual and family morality in a country. Contraception has been shown to be a factor destructive of family, and even social, morality. Natural family planning, on the contrary, is a factor in moral, religious, individual, and social mobilization. To those to whom contraception appears easier than natural family planning, Jesus' words must be recalled: "Make your way in by the narrow gate. It is a broad gate and a wide road that leads on to perdition; and those who go in that way are many indeed; but how small is the gate, how narrow the road that leads on to life, and how few there are that find it" (Mt 7:13-14).

DOCTRINE AND METHOD IN THE PREPARATION OF AND ACTION BY WORKERS IN THE PASTORAL CARE OF MARRIAGE

WANDA AND ANDRZEJ PÓLTAWSKI
(Poland)

Before considering the theme of this paper, we must state some reservations:

1. Obviously, such an extensive theme has to be dealt with in a condensed manner. Therefore, we only intend to make an outline and not a full development of the subject.

2. Since our presentation is addressed to the members of the Pontifical Council for the Family, we assume that all are familiar with the relevant documents of the Holy See and accept their content. Our report does not intend to be polemical. It is an attempt to summarize the results of many years' experience with family pastoral work and to shed light on some of the more urgent problems.

3. In principle, when speaking of a married couple, we mean a couple united by the sacrament. We purposely exclude problems of the divorced and all other types of partnership. Our task here is to prepare a program for the work of Catholic pastoral care of families in order to help married couples achieve the aim foreseen for them by God himself: the sanctification of marriage and the family, with the help of the Church.

In the Encyclical *Humanae Vitae*, Pope Paul VI, in speaking to lay people, expresses his concern about the endangered human family. At present, the human family needs help, and Paul VI asks different groups of people—scientists, physicians, nurses, teachers, but, in the first place, married couples—to offer this help. The Pope speaks about a new form of the apostolate, an apostolate of lay people, in which equals serve their equals: young people serve young people, married couples serve other married couples. What is, in fact, the apostolate of lay people?

It is nothing more than assuming responsibility for the fate of other people, the fate of humanity, and the fate of the Catholic Church. If the family is endangered today, it is precisely because contemporary men and women do not fully assume responsibility for themselves and for their families.

What, then, does "assuming responsibility" mean? To be responsible is to be aware of the fact that I can influence my fate and that of the world, and that this fate depends on my actions. Knowing that, I act in such a way that my actions will bear good fruits and, ultimately, lead to salvation because a believer's responsibility is not limited to the events of this world. A believer's responsibility includes the eternal dimension of the Last Things. A conscious and mature Christian is fully responsible only when his actions aim at sanctity and when they are meant to help others in their striving for sanctity. The current crisis of basic values, including the crisis of marriage and the family, flows precisely from such a lack of responsibility.

Indifference toward the Last Things and toward one's neighbor is growing among contemporary people. People in the twentieth century consume their lives with incomprehensible carelessness, without taking into account the reality of death or the realism of faith, which speaks about the judgment each one has to face. This carelessness flows, on the one hand, from a lack of maturity, and, on the other hand, from a lack of faith. Contemporary man, if he is not an atheist, is nevertheless influenced to such an extent by atheism that faith is something on the fringe of life for him, a traditional ornament. Faith does not influence his life. It is not the driving force of his life. In this way, man loses his own self. He loses the meaning of his existence, seeks sham values which he then wears out or discards in order to seek further. He is still caught up in the restless turmoil of seeking something, and he does not know what it is he is really seeking. In his relationships with other people, he lacks the basic value of love. The selfish search for one's own pleasure does not leave room for the altruistic love of neighbor. The contemporary world and the human family suffer from this lack of love and charity.

Consciously to assume responsibility means looking away from oneself and turning both horizontally toward one's neighbor and vertically toward God, the Creator. Without taking this transcendent dimension into consideration, it is impossible to find oneself and rescue endangered humanity.

Who is responsible for the fate of humanity? Everyone, all mature people, but, in the first place, those who believe in God—the Church as God's people—and, in a special way, people chosen as collaborators of their pastors: the members of the Pontifical Council for the Family and all who work in counseling services for the family. Moreover, this work can be successful only when a counselor knows the real situation and when the advice given reveals the truth.

I. THEORETICAL FOUNDATIONS OF PASTORAL WORK

We do not, of course, wish to repeat the articles of the Creed and the catechism here. However, we will stress those points which many Catholics find difficult to accept, even though they are part of Catholic ethics.

The Church has presented ethical norms in a clear and unequivocal way. It would seem that, in principle, it would be enough for those who consider themselves Catholics to be obedient to them. Pastoral practice demonstrates, however, that observation of these norms in married life and in human sexuality in general is especially difficult.

It seems possible to identify three groups of people who do not observe the norms of Catholic ethics, although they consider themselves Catholics in various ways.

1. The first group is composed of those who pass judgment on the "restrictive ethics of Catholicism" and on the documents of the Church. They do not, however, have any in-depth knowledge about these norms or documents. They are simply a group of indifferent people with superficial convictions formed largely by the mass media. They lack religious knowledge. They may be helped through proper education and real familiarity with Church documents. This group suffers more from ignorance than contestation.

2. A second group of people knows the teaching of the Church but chooses from it what pleases them, while questioning what, for some reason, does not. This is Catholicism à la carte, to be chosen from. These people lack goodwill and true commitment to the Faith. It is a problem of conversion and recognizing the authority of God and the Church.

3. Finally, there is a third group of people, who are perhaps most in need of pastoral care. They recognize that Catholic ethical norms are beautiful. They know exactly what the

Church teaches, but they feel subjectively unable to lead their personal lives according to these norms. If not for their whole personal lives, then for some particular cases, they would like to obtain relief, and they demand it from the Church. Sometimes they demand a change in the norms in the name of charity, love, the good of mankind, etc. These people lack, most of all, the right idea about God himself and of contact with him. The way to help them is above all by enlivening their sacramental life because only the Holy Spirit and sacramental grace can overcome their weaknesses.

To whichever group individuals and whole nations belong, it is obvious that contemporary Catholics encounter special difficulties in accepting the norms of Catholic ethics. In order to understand why this takes place, it is first necessary to mention the norms which cause these difficulties. In the light of experience, we can list the following:

1. The ethical norms about general sexual behavior. The clearly formulated Sixth and Ninth Commandments, repeated in the document *Persona Humana*, exclude sexual activity for all except married people. Only married couples have the right to sexual activity. All others have the duty to preserve their virginity all their lives. The Sixth Commandment is binding for everyone, not just some. This prohibitive norm is universal and, at the same time, is universally contested.

2. The sacramentality of marriage is more and more often questioned to such an extent that not only married couples themselves but even some theologians and pastors undermine the meaning of the Sacrament by, for instance, proposing the equal right to receive the Eucharist of married couples sacramentally united and those who have broken their sacramental union, substituting a civil contract. Many Catholics are not aware of the difference between a legal

contract between two people and a sacramental alliance of two people with God himself.

3. The norm requiring lifelong married union is often disputed, and our contemporaries find a host of arguments which treat lifelong fidelity as something so exceptional that it almost requires heroism.

4. The above causes, or is caused by, rejecting monogamy and marital fidelity. Although monogamy remains the principle for contracting a valid marital union, at the same time there exists the possibility of breaking one contract and going on to another one. This enables a successive passing from one contract to another, which becomes in fact a successive polygamy or polyandry. The legal codes of particular countries do not limit the number of divorces and subsequent new contracts which are possible.

5. The univocal norm of the Fifth Commandment—"You shall not kill"—which is so clear, especially regarding unborn children, has not only been questioned by individuals but has even been legally erased through the legalization of murdering unborn children. What is incomprehensible is that Catholics seem to accept this also.

This questioning of the fundamental right to life leads to violations of the rights of the person as such. All sorts of manipulation of the person then become possible, beginning with manipulation of fecundation up to euthanasia, all performed in the name of the so-called progress of science.

The norm transmitted by the Church is unequivocal: every conceived child, whether well or ill, born or still unborn, is a human being, created in the image of God. It is forbidden to kill or manipulate a child, regardless of the child's age or situation.

6. Lastly, the teaching of the Church is rejected when it indicates how a married couple should be responsible for the

great gift of transmitting life. Not many Catholics, unless they have deep faith and great sensitivity, understand why both artificial fertilization and artificial sterilization are an abuse of rights which do not belong to the person and are sins against the First Commandment. The same applies to contraception. Many others, however, do not seem to understand that artificial fertilization is not the right cure for infertility and may not be treated as such.

II. METHODS OF CONVEYING THE RIGHT ATTITUDE

The aim of this meeting is to coordinate the work of Catholic organizations and movements with individual research and initiative. This is necessary in order to curtail the growing contraceptive attitude and permissive ethics which prevail in almost all the world. Two opposing attitudes, one for life and for the child, and another against life and against the child, are now hanging in the balance. Many, however, who struggle against abortion propagate contraception, not understanding that both are the result of the same contraceptive attitude. Some initiatives for fighting against abortion, also among Catholics, promote contraception as a "remedy" to abortion, but this does not diminish the existing evil. Another problem is that, among specialists and counselors who promote the correct natural methods of regulating fertility, there sometimes exist painful misunderstandings which waste a great deal of energy and reduce the chance of success. The present meeting of persons of goodwill with experience in this field should contribute toward resolving this problem. It would greatly aid the pastoral work of the Catholic Church, whose goal is precisely the salvation of humanity through the sanctification of the family.

The only way to achieve these results is to unite all our forces, create a common "battlefront", and accept an identical program of pastoral activity. In order to do this, we must first clarify and unify certain concepts, and then draw up a common program.

Some existing confusion is partly the fault of priests and doctors who show a lack of precision in their publications. They use popular terms which falsify reality or, at least, lead to general confusion. Here are some examples of the most frequently used terms that cause trouble:

1. "Birth control"

Catholics use this term in many publications, forgetting that birth control can also mean abortion since it excludes birth. Speaking precisely, if one wishes to speak of control, one should speak perhaps about conception control, but this is not an accurate concept either. In reality, man cannot decide about human life and correct God the Creator. Man can control only his own activity, the results of which can affect a child's destiny. It would be better to speak about self-control in sexual activity. This concept is more accurate. From the Christian point of view, knowing that each child is conceived through God's action and the parents' cooperation, the most suitable term seems to be *responsible parenthood*.

The term *birth control* should be eliminated also for a second reason. Essentially, a human being can never direct conception, which occurs by itself. A human being can only prepare the conditions which are propitious to conception or which are not. Whether conception will occur or not is always a mystery. Every doctor knows very well that there are cases in which all the conditions have been fulfilled and, in theory, conception could occur, and yet it does not. A Catholic doctor should believe in the divine origin of the human being and, so to speak, "let God's creative power work". A human being has the possibility and duty of becoming acquainted with the laws of nature that direct human fertility. Without this knowledge, one cannot be fully responsible. That is why the term *responsible parenthood* seems to be the only accurate one.

2. "Methods of directing fertility, of family planning, of birth control"

The next misunderstanding arises from use of the term *methods of directing fertility*. This term is essentially wrong because no method can ever direct human fertility. The human being directs his own actions using different methods. What is more, some Catholic doctors have published both contraceptive and natural methods under one heading, "Methods of Controlling Fertility". In the publications of prominent Catholic doctors, we find tables of the so-called efficacy of all the known methods. They are enumerated one after another. Of course, this makes it difficult to understand why some methods are forbidden, while others are allowed by the Church, if they all have the same goal of not having children.

Such opinions are widespread. They are expressed not only by atheists and enemies of the Church but also by Catholics, even by some priests, and, surprisingly, by some bishops.

In order to avoid such interpretations, it is absolutely necessary to speak of natural methods quite separately, not mentioning them together with contraceptives. The argument that information must be provided about all methods is false. A doctor has not only the right but also the duty to inform people about what he considers right (*Humanae Vitae*, no. 27).

Furthermore, one must remember that natural methods, as opposed to contraceptive methods, have no influence on fertilization. They are only diagnostic methods which show the actual state of the organism. Perhaps it would be better to speak of *diagnostic* methods instead of natural methods and describe them separately. Otherwise, another dangerous misunderstanding arises. Many people speak and write about "artificial" and "natural conception". Such formulations appear also in Catholic publications, and, again, it is difficult to understand why "natural contraception" is permitted and "artificial contraception" prohibited since the latter is the result of medical progress.

3. The "efficacy" of methods of fertility control

The next problem is also a result of describing both "natural and artificial methods" together. It is the problem of the method's so-called efficacy. Personally, I think it is necessary to stop publishing tables presenting percentages of efficacy for all methods because they are the cause of dangerous confusion.

Of course, it is possible to speak about the efficacy of contraceptive means (although, personally, I would prefer to speak of their degree of harmfulness because sometimes efficacy means simply killing the child) because that efficacy does exist. The action of contraceptive means consists essentially in influencing the organism directly, which may be statistically expressed. However, this is true with reference to artificial contraceptive means only. Note that the term *artificial* is not necessary with reference to contraception because it is always artificial. No human organism ever produces any contraceptives by natural means. The term *artificial* became necessary when "natural contraception" was introduced. (One even finds the expression "natural Catholic contraception".)

With regard to the diagnostic methods, the concept of "efficacy" is not only of no use but also has no meaning. There is no action on the organism, and, therefore, one cannot measure the percentage of efficacy. The concept of the "efficacy" of natural methods apparently is used to give the publications describing them a scientific character. Science today, as is well known, uses statistics constantly, but in this particular case they do not adhere to the truth. It seems that modern doctors, even Catholic ones, are afraid to state simply in their scientific writings that if a couple refrains from sexual activity during the woman's fertile period, there is always 100 percent "efficacy", and they can be absolutely sure that no child will be conceived.

With the natural methods, there is no place for counting percentages. What, then, are our colleagues counting when they give the percentage of efficacy of natural methods? Perhaps it would be possible to count the percentage of persons who accept the need for continence during the woman's fertile period. Stating only a "percentage of efficacy", however, does not explain anything. It only raises doubts about the exactness of the diagnostic methods.

Quoting statistics is useful only when the author explains in detail what they represent. For example, the author should say how many couples do not refrain from intercourse on a fertile day although they have decided to do so. In that case, the "disappointment" would concern the couple's attitude and cannot be given as proof of the "inefficacy of the method". In any case, statistics cannot be quoted exclusively which show the "percentage of efficacy" because they falsify the entire situation and cause an unwarranted lack of confidence in the diagnostic methods.

4. Periodic continence

In their publications, Catholics usually stress the need for periodic continence in order to achieve responsible parenthood. This is true, but such a formulation immediately meets with psychological resistance because people think that they are being deprived of and forbidden something. It would seem more effective to stress that periodic continence, or periodicity in general, is the basic principle of human sexual activity.

Apart from the problem of fertility, every married couple is limited in their activity by several factors. Therefore, every human couple has their own rhythm, which depends on many factors, and one of these, although not the only one, must be taking into consideration the rights and the destiny of a child. Periodic continence is necessary not only for responsible parenthood but, and even more so, for preserving fidelity. We would like to stress that periodic continence is the only way to remain faithful to one another. Any sexual activity can and should be subordinated to higher values. Only then does it become truly human. The argument that directing sexual activity is against its spontaneity is contrary to common sense and practice. In reality, human sexual activity can never be totally spontaneous: it is always planned and carried out in concrete, prepared circumstances.

Instead of speaking about the duty or need for periodic continence, it might be better to speak about the choice of the right moment for the loving meeting. It is not true that planning is against spontaneity. Quite the opposite: it heightens the intensity of the experience. Lovers make their appointments for a given day and hour. There is no reason why married couples should not make appointments for that great moment. A new, positive way of speaking about these matters in an encouraging way must be found. We are not trying to make a couple avoid sexual intercourse. We only want them to plan it, to be able to express their love more and more deeply. The sexual act of a married couple is in God's plan for them. In order to attain this dimension, they must find the best moment for experiencing it most deeply.

5. "The unwanted child", "the undesired pregnancy", "preventing pregnancy"

We find such expressions in many publications. They should be excluded, however, from Catholic literature.

No child in reality is ever really "unwanted". Conception takes place through the cooperation of God and the parents. Even if a couple does not want a child who is already conceived, it is obvious that the Creator, who is omnipotent love, cannot call a new life into existence against his will. So, every child is loved by God from the beginning. Every child is also a child of God, not only of humans. A child should be called "God's gift" and not an "unwanted child".

However, it is not true that a child who is "unwanted" will always continue to be unwanted after it is born. Often a child born from a so-called undesired pregnancy is loved more than other children. Therefore, it would be better to say an "unexpected pregnancy", instead of an "undesired pregnancy". A woman may be surprised by her pregnancy, although this surprise may prove to be a lack of responsibility because adults should foresee the effects of their actions. The surprise itself, however, does not mean that the child is "unwanted". Pregnancy is a long process during which a woman's psychology undergoes changes. During the first weeks, the woman may not want the child, but later, especially when she feels the child's movements, she is ready to accept and love the child.

The doctor should not speak of an "unwanted pregnancy", especially because the woman's attitude toward her pregnancy depends very much on his position. Unfortunately, we know very well that often the decision to kill the child is the result of the doctor's negative influence who instead of reassuring the pregnant woman, immediately proposes abortion.

The expression *pregnancy prevention* should never be used because pregnancy is not a disease. One should say "choosing the best possible moment for the birth of the next child".

6. "Artificial abortion"

It is clear that abortion must be named in some way. I think, however, that if every doctor and every Catholic, in private and official conversations or publications, expressed this truth by its real name, in many cases the life of a child could be saved in this simple way. If we addressed ourselves to doctors saying, "How many children have you killed today?" I think there might be greater sensitivity. Circumspect language used in these cases causes increased indifference. No one is surprised today by the infamous fact that contemporary medicine often serves death instead of life.

III. TEACHING DIAGNOSTIC METHODS

Apart from the problem of unifying what we say and write, the problem remains of the choice and evaluation of the various diagnostic methods. The adherents of so-called natural family planning sometimes seem to forget that the solution to the problem lies not in the choice of method but in the attitude of the couple to be ready to accept some discipline in their married life. This attitude is most important. Pastoral experience shows that people who have the right attitude will always find the right method. However, it is very difficult to teach a biological method to people who have the wrong contraceptive attitude. A diagnostic method may always be changed because medicine is constantly offering new information, but what is difficult to change is the attitude. Therefore, in pastoral work, it is very important to teach not only diagnostic methods but ethics as well.

It is also necessary to be well versed in the various biological, diagnostic methods and to teach them without discrimination. Some methods cause psychological or esthetic resistance, and there are also cultural differences. Therefore, tact is required and the choice must be left to the couple. Diagnostic methods in themselves are morally indifferent. They only acquire moral value through the intention of the act and accompanying circumstances. Therefore, it cannot be said that one method is morally good and another evil. They may be qualified according to other criteria—for instance, that one is simple and another complicated. However, it is necessary to remember that because the diagnostic methods in themselves are morally indifferent, no one should be judged for using one method or another.

IV. PASTORAL INITIATIVES

The Church has always tried to educate people and help them on their way to salvation. But, in our times, it seems necessary to take special care of the family because of the growing crisis.

It is impossible to enumerate every type of initiative. We can only outline some of our own experiences and stress that there are numerous possibilities for lay people to cooperate with their pastors.

1. Teaching children the right meaning of sexuality.
2. Organizing meetings with youth and discussing the problems of virginity, chastity, and Catholic ethics as distinguished from permissive ethics.
3. Marriage-preparation courses, including biological methods.
4. Counseling centers and courses for married couples.
5. Organizing religious exercises in connection with liturgical feasts: Christmas, Lent, etc.
6. Organizing special meetings for people who have just baptized their children. (Information about biological methods is particularly needed at this time because fertility must be monitored during the breastfeeding period.)
7. Organizing meetings with physicians and nurses to confront their professional ethics with Catholic principles, encouraging them to collaborate with pastors, and give them information about biological, diagnostic methods, which is often lacking.
8. Meetings with students, in particular of medicine and theology.
9. Collaboration with religious orders, particularly in defense of the unborn child.
10. Helping with the adoption of children.
11. Organizing vacations for family circles.

The basic program of the meetings should be the same—Catholic ethics, general and sexual—only the manner of speaking must be adapted to the audience: e.g., children, married couples. Persons who decide to be active in family pastoral work not only must know the teaching of the Church and related topics but also must be aware of their responsibility for the results of their work. The role of a counselor (or member of this council) requires a particular attitude and commitment. It is obvious that people who undertake these tasks must be properly prepared for them, perhaps through specialized courses.

V. THE TASKS OF FAMILY PASTORAL WORKERS

The situation described here indicates that the tasks awaiting family pastoral workers are not easy. The persons who wish to undertake them must be aware of their grave responsibility. In order really to collaborate with pastors, they must:

1. Know the doctrine of the Church and accept the norms of Catholic ethics regarding sexual and married life without reservations. Moreover, they must understand that the ethical norms of the Church can never be changed and that they do not allow for compromise. Catholic ethics must be totally accepted or rejected. This does not mean that a Catholic never sins or never transgresses ethical norms. It does mean, however, that a Catholic must call evil by its true name, sin, and try to change his ways if and when he sins.

2. Accepting ethics is not only a verbal declaration but also a way of life. Whoever decides to work in family pastoral care must observe the ethical norms in his own life. This life must give witness not only to his own faith but also to the fact that these norms are possible to live by. To

achieve this, the believer must continuously check his own convictions in the light of the doctrine of the Church. In pastoral work, all counseling must agree with the teaching of the Church. The Catholic Faith is founded on God's authority, and that cannot be opposed. It is the only sure foundation on which man can build.

In *Humanae Vitae*, Paul VI speaks about science which is in accordance with faith and right reason. The believer who knows who God is and who man is must try to achieve this accordance of faith, reason, and life. Not every science is in accordance with faith, and not every reason is right. One must be aware of one's own limits: the limits of one's own reasoning, the limits of science. If someone thinks that there is a discrepancy between faith and science, is unable to understand the demands of the Church, there is only one way out: to accept what the Church teaches with deep humility. The greatest dangers to humanity derive from the sin of hubris, the pride of man who wants to be like God and to decide about human destiny.

3. The value system of Catholic ethics is not always recognized in the contemporary world. Those who have the courage to accept it must be independent of the pernicious opinions of their surroundings and must be able to oppose current trends resolutely.

Part Two
REPORTS

MEDICAL PERSONNEL AND NATURAL FAMILY PLANNING

JOHN AND LORNA BERGIN
(New Zealand)

We address the topic of medical personnel and natural family planning at the conceptual level because that is the level at which we have studied and debated it over a long period of time. We have not dealt very much with the day-to-day clinic teaching, testing one technique against another, but we have used the method, have had discussions with many others who have used it, and have been closely associated with doctors heavily involved in practical teaching as well as with married women leaders in New Zealand's special teacher-trainee program. We believe that we are speaking "from the data of human science and the experience of married couples".

The goodness of the method

We have long held the view that natural family planning, although not free from the possibility of abuse, is intrinsically and abundantly good; that it is not something that is merely tolerable but has built-in values which facilitate personal growth, mutual respect, dialogue, and communion. By contrast we have long felt that artificial contraception, to which natural family planning is the preferred alternative, is disruptive of design, destroys self-giving, denies the dignity of making mutual but independent decisions for each act of intercourse, and is linked to more disaster than it averts (immaturity, infidelity, infection, neoplasia, sterility, abortion).

We are aware of the affirmation in recent and earlier papal teaching of these views—the insistence that continence is neither contradiction nor contraception; that persons not bodies make love; that responsible parenthood through natural family planning is more than capitalizing on convenient cycles of fertility; that the ideal interaction of husband and wife combines the spiritual with the psychological and biological. We see the Church as cherishing the best in sexual activity rather than oppressing married people. We do not believe that the grass is greener on the other side of the fence.

Medical personnel and natural family planning

From that background we offer our reflections on medical personnel and natural family planning. In doing so we look at medical personnel across the board, not just Catholic medical personnel. In making that distinction we immediately confront one of the problems in presenting natural family planning as the ideal means to responsible parenthood. I [John] refer to the view widely held that natural family planning is something discovered and promoted by Catholics for themselves, just another method of contraception which some of them use. Such views will not motivate doctors at large to be interested, and even many Catholic medical people have an incomplete view of the task with which they have been asked to assist. What is that task? It is to evangelize the world of marriage and family with a method of spacing children that is compatible with the nature of men and women, will do no harm, and overflows with positive values. No one will spread this message unless he believes it, nor will it go far enough if it is seen as something for Catholics rather than an ideal for mankind. It will not go very far unless the teacher shares our insights about the contribution of periodic continence to human conduct and personal development.

To date a relatively small number of doctors have taken a prominent or persevering part in promoting natural family planning, and although they are nearly all Catholics, they represent a minority of Catholic doctors. There have been a small number of very able medical men and women who have made original observations at the clinical and laboratory level, conducted early trials, and observed the changes required for success. Some have worked in association with biochemists and endocrinologists making hormone measurements that have validated observations about temperature variations and mucus changes. They have built the platforms from which other doctors have moved to lead the development in their own countries. Further out in the circle are those Catholic obstetricians and family physicians who are faithful to magisterial teaching, advise their own patients appropriately, and play their part in teaching nonmedical assistants to teach others. Although all this has been encouragingly successful in some regions and countries, natural family planning is not a gift to be confined to Catholics, and there remains a big harvest needing many laborers. On present indications, however, there is little likelihood that there will be enough convinced and active medical personnel to meet the need even among Catholics for instructors of their own. This encompasses a twofold problem. On the one hand many Catholic doctors, possibly the majority, are not yet completely dedicated to the magisterial teaching on responsible parenthood and may act at least in regard to the pill in a way little different from those with other philosophical bases. A first task is to strengthen the understanding of our own.

I am aware that it may seem contradictory to point out that natural family planning is essentially physiological, not essentially Catholic, and then call for more Catholic medical personnel who will take part in the work. The reason is that up to now most of the teaching and guiding in this field have been in Catholic hands and most of the demand has been from Catholic patients. Moreover, Pope John Paul II made the point in the reflections we have been studying for this meeting that members of the Church—and that must include medical members—should appreciate more readily the theology and ethics of periodic continence because in addition to natural law they have the Church. Pope Paul VI outlined the natural-law argument; Pope John Paul II has supplemented this with the pedagogy of the language of the body, which he sees as biblical and revealed.

Competence and availability

The second problem about Catholic personnel—or for that matter any medical personnel—is that when they *have* become convinced and willing, they do not have the time to deal in a relaxed and extended way with the numbers, or the hoped for numbers, of those wanting instruction. For this reason and for others, the details of the learning process, temperature, and mucus are really better dealt with by the trained woman teacher. Certainly we have found this so in New Zealand, as Lorna will tell you shortly.

Does this mean that there is not such a real need for

converted physicians as I have implied? There certainly remains a need for the doctor first to validate the whole concept, next to introduce the couple to a learning situation, and most of all to support their decision to adopt natural family planning and their effort to work their way through it. The doctor should also be available to help with difficult training situations and when pregnancy occurs contrary to expectation.

When all is said and done, and we count the Catholics who seek and practice natural family planning and others whose motivation is not theological who have joined them, the number reached by natural family planning teachers is relatively small. Although in natural family planning we have a precious gift which we would willingly share, we do not see the divine plan coming toward fulfillment until recognition of the natural law leads men and women in general to use these methods of birth regulation. This is unlikely to happen without a major change of heart among doctors whose basic philosophy is secular and utilitarian.

In *Humanae Vitae* Pope Paul VI addressed himself to men of goodwill. He also said, "We believe that our contemporaries are particularly capable of seeing that this teaching is in harmony with human reason." Events have shown that Pope Paul was unduly optimistic as far as both doctors and the public at large are concerned. In *Familiaris Consortio* Pope John Paul II spoke with equal hope but perhaps less expectation when he said, "In the context of a culture which seriously distorts or entirely misinterprets the true meaning of sexuality (because it separates it from its essential reference to the person), the Church more urgently feels how irreplaceable is her mission of presenting sexuality as a value and a task of the whole person." What Pope John Paul II is referring to when he speaks of "the culture which seriously distorts" is surely the *contraceptive mentality*, and our experience is that most doctors have this as much as the general public; in fact, doctors foster it.

Understanding and confidence

It is my belief that among the general run of doctors there is little understanding of or desire for natural family planning and no confidence in it. Catholic women who have sought help in this area will confirm what I say. The matter is of importance because most women, Catholic or not, do not have easy access to a doctor who has adopted the ideals of *Humanae Vitae* or *Familiaris Consortio*, and most women wanting assistance with fertility regulation begin their search with their family doctor. Those women genuinely seeking a morally acceptable method of family limitation are not going to find easily the help they are seeking, and the very large number of women who would consider, and some of whom would use, natural family planning if they knew about it—or if it were presented to them—will never have this opportunity until medical practitioners at large undergo a major conversion. I am not dreaming of a mass religious conversion, although philosophy and ethics are at the heart of the problem, but of an openness which would at least remove denigration, see something of the values inherent in natural family planning over and above limitation of family size, and offer it as a viable option, or at the very least assist a couple who have expressed a preference in favor of it.

I have said doctors are unaware of natural family planning or, if they are aware of it, lack confidence in it or in the people planning to use it. This is partly because it has not been presented to them with power and polish; partly because they are not eager to listen; partly because they regard the exercise as a Catholic peculiarity akin to the unwillingness of Jehovah's Witnesses to receive blood transfusions; partly because they have had experience of women who have used natural family planning unsuccessfully; partly because they have not seen enough scientifically convincing reports of the efficacy of the method and do not really accept the distinctions between method failure, teacher failure, and patient failure. But if doctors are exposed to convincing studies, they still have difficulties with prejudice, with a belief that medical treatment is being prescribed by the Pope, and their anxiety is heightened if patients are attending a Church-related clinic with instruction coming from nonmedical personnel. The remedy for this is somehow to increase the liaison between the medical and nonmedical personnel so that they work more closely together.

The fundamental error

In addition to these various factors the basic one is that the secular-oriented doctor in this field is set on a method from which he expects no child and that is the limit of his expectation. Marriage building and personal growth through periodic continence are not his primary concern partly because so many of those for whom contraceptives are supplied are in any case not in a regular marital situation, while mention of "conjugal chastity or the language of the body expressed reciprocally in the integral truth of its meaning" would indeed be a foreign language for those with no background of metaphysics.

It is rare to hear of a doctor who is not a magisterially adherent Catholic who is vigorously promoting natural family planning. Among medical personnel help might have been expected or sought from Christian physicians of other denominations, but in my experience this is rarely forthcoming. I take this to be because the Protestant ethic, based so directly on Scripture, finds little there which seems to outlaw contraception, and to some extent the same applies to abortion. The recently offered insights from the Holy Father about the theology of the body based on revelation could perhaps place a new perspective before Protestant colleagues, but again it is an optimistic missionary who sees the average Protestant doctor studying Pope John Paul II for guidelines on family planning. It is here that those of us who are doctors must expose the wisdom of the teaching to our colleagues if and when we can. Before we Catholics can proclaim, however, we must attend to our development, and there should be no relaxation in the pastoral dialogue with our own medical personnel.

Advertising or attitude?

It has been suggested to me that we could influence doctors sceptical about natural family planning by better scientific publications, by better promotion in drug-company style, or by the development of a new technology, something that would enable a woman to press a button on her watch and read the basal body temperature or even the word *go*. The argument is that doctors and patients are so attuned to the technical in medicine that something like this would sell. My own experience of difficulty in getting doctors as well as journalists to accept facts that they do not wish to believe, like the humanity of the zygote, makes me sceptical. I think it is a change of heart, a change of attitude that is required, a change that will lead the doctor to see beyond the womb or the vas and look at the couple in a holistic manner—and medicine is not holistic unless it includes the spiritual—with thoughts of preserving the gifts of fertility, so that men and women make gifts of themselves as people or as integral human beings.

If natural family planning is to be extended, and especially if it is to be extended among that section of the community that has not yet heard of it or been encouraged to give it serious consideration, there is still a big task in promotion, promotion which must present it for what it is—something much greater than avoidance of pregnancy. The promotion needs to be to people generally, but medical personnel are key figures in encouraging or at least not discouraging. They have to see natural family planning in "data from sciences and from the experience of married couples". The data from the sciences will have to be provided by the medical and paramedical among us who are believers, but conversion may come from the experience of married couples, what the patients teach the doctors, and at this point Lorna will add her light to what I have said.

Training personnel in natural family planning

We have been asked to speak on medical personnel and natural family planning, and Jack has done this, but he has also indicated that the picture is incomplete without reference to those who work alongside medical personnel—women and couples whom doctors and others instruct. In fact most of the work in New Zealand is done by married women and couples, although in some parts of the Pacific religious women also are teachers.

Our teacher training involves women who are trained in depth, who attend a residential period of instruction, and who receive, eventually, formal certification. The courses for training are financed from government funds, which is not the case in all countries. There were originally problems as to whether such funding would be granted, as there was reluctance on the part of the Health Department to support a selective form of family planning. Eventually what won the day was an argument totally in line with what Pope John Paul II has said repeatedly—that is, that natural family planning is more than birth regulation, that it is a form of marriage building. Because of this support for marriage and its growth, funds were made available from the Family Health Division of the Department of Health.

In addition to training natural family planning teachers, a new departure is the training of educators in the philosophy of natural family planning so that a much wider audience is reached and hopefully influenced.

The advantage of women teachers who are fully aware of their own sexuality and fertility patterns is that they can relate better to other women than can male doctors. Women doctors would have a particular qualification for this work. Because, too, lay women can deal in a more relaxed way with their clients, the women are more at ease and don't feel they are taking up too much of the time of a busy doctor. The work is an apostolate—those who have taken it on have fully justified their call—but most medical personnel are still to be convinced of the acceptability and efficacy of natural family planning. Jack has mentioned the challenge that this presents to Catholic doctors who are working in this area. In a paradoxical way too I know that it is sometimes women users of the method who have taught the doctors of its success in a way that their own colleagues have not been able to do. After all it is women who have persuaded doctors to allow husbands to be present right at the delivery of their babies, women who have promoted the return of breastfeeding, and it may yet be women who convince doctors that natural family planning does work and that those who use it are happy in their married love.

Continued support

It is really love that is being taught to clients and it is love that we are trying to teach the doctors. One way to do this is to be available to help when despite instruction in natural family planning a pregnancy occurs, or indeed when a planned pregnancy causes difficulties. This is where pregnancy support groups such as Pregnancy Help or Birthright have a very important part to play. They have often come into existence because of the prevalence of abortion in a country, but our own groups in New Zealand have worked hard to be pro-life in the widest sense. Pregnancy Help offers any woman or girl distressed in any way because of her pregnancy a twenty-four-hour service. It may be friendship, counseling, or just a listening ear that is needed; it may be practical help with housework or child-minding or a home for an unmarried mother, but whatever it is hopefully shows something of Christ's love for those in need. Hopefully too medical personnel may have less reason to complain about a pregnancy which they may feel is just an affliction for the woman and themselves if they know there is some back-up available.

There is one other aspect of natural family planning which may or may not involve medical personnel, and that is the teaching of fertility awareness to the young. Just as training of women teachers is better done by women users of the method there is much to be said for married women or couples being teachers of young people who are still some time away from marriage. At this stage what we contemplate is imparting not only an awareness of fertility patterns—the fragility of their fertility—but an awareness of the part of that fertility pattern in the divine plan. On this base and a Christian background long-term aspects of relationship and vocation can be built. We are not teaching natural family planning for use or experimentation by young people; we are giving them knowledge about their bodies which should make them appreciate their own gifts and about their persons which should enable them to use those gifts prudently, generously, and virtuously in the future. Natural family planning falls short if it is not incorporated as a building element in Christian marriage.

Conclusion

We have briefly contrasted natural family planning and artificial contraception, the former physiological rather than Catholic. Medical personnel with knowledge and experience of this gift have a special task to evangelize the world with a method of child spacing that is harmless and beneficial. To achieve this we have to be not only sure of the best possible presentation but also aware of the hurdles erected by the contraceptive mentality, secular and religious, by the sales pressure for drugs and devices, and by the false doctrine and fierce prejudice that oppose us in medical and social circles. A heavy responsibility in fulfilling this task falls to doctors, especially the doctors of this council, and other Catholic doctors, to the work of chosen women teachers, and to the cooperation of the clergy with all these groups.

TRANSMISSION OF APOSTOLIC SENSITIVITY INSIDE AND OUTSIDE THE HOME

ROBERTO AND ELIZABETH DE LA FUENTE
(Mexico)

I. The family's mission

What is the family's mission? What is its role in God's plan? We will speak of what the family is and not what its functions are in order to avoid confusion.

There are various aspects of the family:

1. The family is called to be a space and environment where the love of the spouses grows and is manifested. The family is where spouses give affection, understanding, support, and guidance. It is the place and space where both need one another for their whole lives because they would not be able to grow and be happy if they were not together. Therefore, their love is the source from which their children drink. Children are a very important part of a couple's life, but they are not the reason but the result of their love, and children do not remain in the home forever.

2. The family is called to be a place of personalization. In their parents' arms, children open their eyes to life, they find the satisfaction of their needs; they begin to love others

because they need them, and, little by little, they learn to need them because they love them.

In the family each one has worth as a person. Other persons are discovered, and a love relationship is established with them; in doing so, great joy is experienced because we are all made for love, and in the family one can love and be loved. In the home we all contribute to everyone's formation. The family is everyone's responsibility because each one brings something unique to it.

3. The family is called to be the environment in which values are discovered and transmitted. The most marked aspects of our personality are acquired in the family. Especially during the first years of life it is so beautiful to see how our deepest values are born out of what we learned in the family. In the same way, our most serious shortcomings are a product of the flaws in our family community.

The Second Vatican Council speaks to us about the family community as the school of the richest humanism. What does this mean? When a family makes efforts to integrate itself and carry out its mission, in that home the best attitudes, beliefs, and forms of life which are focused on human interests and values and promote development of the person are lived, understood, and chosen. This is humanism.

4. The family is called to be a place and environment where persons grow and are educated in the Faith. In our family the path that leads us to God also begins. In the family, by living the human experience of being parents and children in a dimension of faith, we are educated in divine paternity, and we learn to live as brothers and sisters. This experience of loving parents, children, and siblings as "another me" then leads to the human community and enables us to love the rest of mankind, to relate to them and experience justice and

solidarity. We, parents, are certainly not the only ones who reveal God because when parents die, children are in need of God, and he will reveal himself to them in other ways.

5. The family is called to be the starting point for integrating its members into social life. The first "others" whom a child meets are his parents, siblings, and relatives. But starting with the family, he begins to relate to other persons: neighbors, friends, parents' relations, etc. This opens a child up little by little toward others.

In order to educate its members properly, a family must be the place where the happenings and the reality of the community, country, and world are observed, commented on, and judged. Parents and children must help one another to discover through this constant observation what God and the community expect from them.

All of the above can be synthesized by saying that the family, as the first center of communion and participation, is both an educator of persons and an educator in the Faith, and, as a result of these two activities, also the promoter of the integral development of the community through its members. The above has been taken from the document of Puebla and Medellín of our Latin American bishops.

Of course, we are speaking about families who have all the elements for carrying out this function. Today, however, the family grows in very adverse conditions.

II. The family's commitment in and toward the community

As Christians, the Church is part of us and we also are a living part of it. The Second Vatican Council tells us that the

Church is both human and divine; Christ is the head and we are its body.

The Holy Spirit unites us as parts of that body through the same Faith, the same sacraments, and the same rule because Christ entrusted Saint Peter and his successors with the care of it as the shepherd cares for his sheep. We who believe in Christ and are part of his body through baptism make up the people of God. We pray and work so that the whole world may become part of that people.

We invite everyone through our words and the example of our lives to recognize Jesus as the author of salvation and principle of unity and peace. All of us who are baptized are called to this mission. We, the laity, are Christ's apostles in the world to bring the salt and light of the gospel where the Church cannot go except through us.

The Council tells us: Let us reflect on Christ's teachings about service. He tells us that, contrary to what is happening in the world, where leaders tyrannize people and the great oppress the weak, we Christians must serve our equals.

If we want to be first, we have to put ourselves in the last place and serve others. Christ supported this teaching by his own example: "Just as the Son of Man came not to be served but to serve, and to give his life as a ransom for many" (Mt 20:25–28).

But before asking us to serve one another, Christ teaches us to love because the deep reason for serving is love. A Christian serves his brothers because he loves them, cares about what happens to them, and wants to see them happy. In this a Christian imitates the Father, who loved us to the point that he sent us his only Son to save us. Whoever imitates Christ finds real nourishment in obedience to the Father's will. Christ not only wanted to serve but enjoyed doing so.

In the Old Testament we find the first commandment to serve given by God to Moses: "You must fear Yahweh your God, you must serve him, by his name you must swear" (Dt 6:13).

Christ told us very clearly that whoever serves one of his brothers is serving him. Let us recall his words when he spoke to us about the day when he would come in glory to judge us: "I was hungry and you gave me food, I was thirsty and you gave me drink; I was a stranger and you made me welcome. . . . Come, you whom my Father has blessed." It is for this reason that in order to keep a true attitude of Christian service, we need to have faith. We need to know that the Lord is among our brothers and sisters and that he wanted to present himself to us in that person who is sad, or imprisoned, or sick. Note that Christ does not tell us: "When you gave your brother to eat or drink it was as if you fed me." He says very clearly: "You gave me food to eat." In seeing all this, we understand why the Lord, when he asks us to carry his yoke, then tells us: "Learn from me, for I am gentle and humble in heart, and you will find rest for your souls! Yes, my yoke is easy and my burden light."

We feel that the first mission of the laity lies primarily in the activities of daily life in the home, at work, with neighbors, and with the different groups to which we belong. The service we give there is personal and spontaneous as needs and occasions present themselves. However, this is not the only service we can lend. In order to attend to major community problems, there are service organizations which coordinate many people's efforts and thereby achieve much greater efficacy.

The parish also offers different areas of service. Other lay apostolate organizations attend to various needs of the community. And there are a host of institutions that attend to the sick and needy, all of which need persons willing to collaborate in their service. In our country, agents for pastoral care of the family are lacking.

At times we think that the problems of the world are too great to be solved. Let us consider what would happen if all the Christians in every country were really to decide to answer their call to serve. In a few years our reality would be changed, and we would also be infinitely better, more optimistic, and happier.

Christ does not ask us to account for everything that happens in the world. But he will surely ask us about what is happening around us: about the hunger we could have satisfied, the injustice we could have impeded, about the hope and love we could have transmitted to our brothers and sisters. Let us begin now to love and serve so that at the end of time Christ's words will resound for us: "Come, you whom my Father has blessed."

PRESENTATION AND RECEPTION OF THE HOLY FATHER'S CATECHESIS

BERNARD AND HUGUETTE FORTIN
(Canada)

The Divine Mission

For the human couple, the transmission of life is both an obvious and a mysterious mission. The obviousness derives from biological complementarity, and the mystery is based precisely on the fact that we, as a couple, become "cooperators" in God the Creator's love. To give life is an unsurpassable responsibility, a mission that places us at the center of God's eternal project, in the plan which God stamped on the humanity of men and women since their creation (cf. FC, no. 28).

The part of the text regarding transmission of life marks the summit of the Apostolic Exhortation's teachings on the duties of the Christian family. After analyzing the family's situation, the text specifies its meaning and mission: service to life, without which service to people, society, and the Church, in the long term, becomes useless and nonexistent.

However, we cannot speak about service to life, an eminently social and community service, without going back to the mission, vocation, and ministry of the couple in God's plan. By going back to this starting point, we are able to understand generosity, openness to life, and society.

Rereading nos. 11, 13, and 14 of *Familiaris Consortio* leads us to marvel at this ministry, as does no. 32. The language of faith and human language enable us to discover that we must reproduce and evince love that is triune, unique, indissoluble, exclusive, and fecund. As sons and daughters of God, brothers and sisters in Christ, God entrusts us from the beginning with our part of the administration of love. This "part" must be based on the image and likeness of God characterized by unity, indissolubility, and fecundity, and on the time and daily life of the couple, as well as their spiritual path in search of holiness. It is in this way that the main objective of the family, of the couple, becomes service to life and love, in its many and complex aspects.

On the other hand, we must act in such a way that this "mission", this "vocation", becomes like the family: that is, what it is. As John Paul II said to the priests of Venice in July 1985: "Conjugal love is not just a commonplace reality. It is the sign that God elevates sacramentally so that spouses truly perceive the ministries of marriage, the first of which is the family. The family is the privileged place where spouses communicate through their own, and not a delegated, vocation."

If we do not have this concern, having children risks becoming an instrumental role considered utilitarian both in society and in the Church. It appears essential to us to take another look and reflect on the "origins", and to unveil the particular charism of the sacrament of marriage: "conjugal love".

The value of the sacrament

Here, in our opinion, is the basic point of our reflection. With great urgency we have to do away with certain narrow viewpoints and show all the mystery, the "greatness, breadth, and depth", of the sacrament of marriage, the sacrament of conjugal love. This conjugal pact is mysterious, but it is also bold and revolutionary in our societies.

A man and a woman are called by God, chosen by God to become signs and reflections of God's triune, faithful love for his people, and of the love pact between Christ and his Church. From the beginning God entrusted a mission, a role, a service to man and woman. He still entrusts us with that ministry, and the common priesthood of all baptized persons, through the sacrament of marriage, becomes distinct but not dissociated from the priesthood of priests and celibates. In this way, it becomes unique and specific, even irreplaceable. Priesthood in conjugal love, this challenge, this madness for the Kingdom, consecrated by God through the sacrament, freely taken on by spouses in uniting themselves definitively to one another with love as their only contract and forgiveness as the privileged means, involves a saving mission, a particular service: the ministry of the family, of the domestic Church (*FC*, no. 49), the ministry of the good news of the family that is one, holy, Catholic, and apostolic.

Men and women today, the present-day Christians who trust in God's plan, need to hear that, by making them ministers of the Sacrament, God—and Christ confirmed this to us—entrusts them with and recognizes their ministry. He assures the presence of the Spirit in their conjugal life; he accompanies them by leaving them the word as nourishment, conjugal love as the gift of the Spirit, and the unquenchable fecundity of triune life. This fecundity thus becomes a richness for the couple, the family, the society, and the Church.

The Synod of 1983 perceived the extraordinary evolution between *Lumen Gentium* and *Familiaris Consortio*, with regard to the language used in speaking about the sacrament of marriage. Our reading of these great texts, without forgetting *Gaudium et Spes*, enables us to state that the sacrament of marriage has all the characteristics of a sacred ministry: that of conjugal love. This ministry enables us to say in our daily lives: "Here is flesh of my flesh" from Genesis, or even "my sister, my love" from the Song of Songs.

Service to life will not be meaningful for Christian spouses unless we, in the Church, with theologians, moralists, canonists, pastors, and couples, are capable of giving the sacrament of marriage the place it deserves, and unless we develop farther our reflection on the meaning and importance of the specific ministry of a man and a woman who decide to accept and respond to the call inviting them to become signs and reflections of triune love.

Signs of hope

However, as beautiful and noble as this vocation to marriage and the transmission of life as cooperators in God the Creator's love may be, we must say that this good news about the family has not been given, in our opinion, the importance it deserves. The lack of enthusiasm that surrounded the publication of *Humanae Vitae*, the tepid promotion of *Familiaris Consortio*, the unwillingness to receive the truth of the Church from "Rome", the increasingly different schools of thought within the same Church, the failure to remember that a pastoral function is also a role of popularization of what one believes, all this paralyzes pastors and the faithful who waste a lot of time looking for what they ought to find immediately and well. Not only does the Tower of Babel apply to the past: it seems to be well built among us also! The North American context, in which a short-sighted humanism is flourishing, does not help things. We can recognize ourselves in the words of the Exhortation regarding the situation of the family in today's world (*FC*, no. 6ff.).

However some signs of hope are coming up on the horizon, and we would like to present them to you:

1. At present, in our diocese of Montreal, we are about to produce a directory of pastoral care of the family which will probably be entitled "Call to the Sacrament of Marriage". Our intention is that all pastoral interventions be made on the basis of the sacrament of Christian marriage: in the school, in the home, in remote, proximate, and immediate marriage preparation, and in our work with persons living in difficult marital situations. It is in this spirit that we are orienting our activities so that the "yes" of spouses will be comparable to the *adsum* of the sacrament of the priesthood.

2. In following John Paul II's invitation to concern ourselves with preparing young people for marriage, we are offering to the engaged who so desire a "catechumenate" for the engaged in which the catecheses of baptism, the Eucharist, confirmation, and the sacrament of Penance are reviewed, and in which the sacrament of marriage is dealt with clearly, as well as its expression in the language of the body. We have also experimented with and presented a text which enables the engaged to take a look at their Christian practice. That text has been submitted in French, English, and Spanish to Edouard Cardinal Gagnon, president of our Council. In it the engaged also learn the importance of service to life and the natural methods of fertility regulation, which they are taught by a couple who use that method.

3. In order to help young couples married for less than five years, especially those who come from the catechumenate,

we organize meetings in which they continuously strive to improve as spouses and learn to be fruitful and happy to be fertile. Some couples have already had their first child, and we marvel at their presence and participation in the life of the Church.

4. For separated or divorced couples, special meetings are held. The abandoned spouse finds comfort there, reawakens awareness of the sacrament, and is convinced that if the other spouse has abandoned his or her conjugal ministry, the other still remains bound to the parental ministry. In all charity, he or she is invited to take care of the children who were brought to life through love. Our present experience in this pastoral area convinces us that a clear presentation of the reality of Christian marriage makes people aware of their responsibilities and of their sacrament.

5. If many couples refuse to transmit life and thereby refuse to take part in God's creative task, the fact remains that many others hesitate because of a society which is not highly receptive to children and is poorly organized in helping those who wish to begin a family. Therefore, we have decided to play an active role with the government of our province, which is drawing up a family policy. All agents of pastoral care of the family and many parishes and organizations have been mobilized so that Christian couples will make their voice heard in this discussion. This action has not been overlooked, and our legislators have felt the prodding of Christian families. A report on these activities has also been given to our president.

6. Our contacts with groups involved in promoting natural family planning have been constant, both on the provincial as well as on the national and international levels. A new

dynamism is noted there which, we hope, will end the heartrending division within our Church in this area.

Family Action

Following the 1980 Synod, the Canadian bishops, with the collaboration of the Knights of Columbus, created an organization called Action Famille (Family Action), while, at the same time, giving priority to pastoral care of the family. This decision enabled publication of two working documents: one on marriage and the family, and another on responsible parenting.

Founded in 1982, Family Action is involved in promoting responsible parenthood. For this purpose it fosters awareness, appreciation, and respectful governing of human fertility, that gift of God whereby each person can participate in the creation of a new human life. It orients its activities especially toward young people and prepares programs aimed at youth and new couples. It pursues its objectives both by supporting already-operating initiatives and by encouraging new ones. It extends its collaboration to Church bodies and other groups or organizations by exchanging information and material resources as well as by offering consultations in the area of leader formation. It is inspired by the teachings of the Roman Catholic Church as defined and presented by the ecclesiastical hierarchy in the light of the recent documents of the Second Vatican Council.

Serena-Canada

Within this perspective of promoting service to life, we must also speak about Serena-Canada, which was founded in

1955. For thirty years, this organization, made up of couples who use the natural family planning method, has been developing educational activities which are in line with and support the Church's thinking in this area. It is interesting to note that Serena-Canada, which has three hundred service centers all over Canada, was created before the Council, before *Gaudium et Spes* and *Humanae Vitae*.

Serena is an educational and aid service specializing in natural planning of the family aimed at developing the couple. It addresses itself mainly to adults but also to young people and adolescents.

It proposes a model of social-development service based on the relationship of like to like, of one couple to another. Being a service with a human dimension, it stresses promotion of man and woman and places techniques at the service of the person. By stimulating couples to be concerned with their own development, Serena goes beyond the application of a technique and sets its sights on all the resources of the human person.

We would also like to mention the growth of the Canadian branch of WOOMB International. This organization promotes one natural method in particular: the ovulation method of Dr. Billings. Within this same perspective, the service Life-Love is carried out in the Quebec area.

Lastly, our experience as a couple during eighteen years of marriage, with three children from ten to seventeen years of age, enables us to appreciate the merits of our Church's teaching on regulating births and service to life. The discovery of this wisdom has directly led us to God and to an ever deeper understanding of his wonderful plan for Christian marriage.

DISSEMINATION OF THE POPE'S CATECHESIS: ITS PUBLICATION, RECEPTION, AND PROBLEMS

NORBERT AND RENATE MARTIN
(Federal Republic of Germany)

In the first part of our intervention, we would like briefly to outline the German situation with regard to the *doctrinal aspects* of the question and problems which concern us here. In the second part, some practical aspects will follow. Both parts will be the background for our observations on the dissemination of the Pope's catechesis, its publication, reception, and problems.

The situation in Germany: theoretical and practical dissent

Undoubtedly, German theology plays an important part in the theological situation of the whole Church. Every notable theologian, if asked his opinion, will admit that German theology is one of the most respected voices in the concert of the universal Church. Furthermore, the German Church possesses an efficient pastoral organization, with its compact network of councils, Catholic organizations, academies, and institutions for adult education. Each diocese (and many of the Catholic organizations) has its own office for marriage and family concerns.

At the same time, Germany is one of the Christian countries where secularization and de-Christianization have made the greatest progress. This is proven by several sociological research studies, the latest of which is the scientific Allensbach investigation entitled "Catholics 1985". Therefore, it is not surprising to see that the divergence between the official teaching of the Church and the practice and subjective opinion of the faithful is extreme, especially in the field of marriage and family ethics. This became clear after the publication of *Humanae Vitae*. This dissent was manifested by the practice of contraception by many couples before the Encyclical and was favored and legitimated by some popular theologians. Confusion was increased by the *Königsteiner Erklärung*, a document of the German Episcopal Conference which is openly misinterpreted as allowing contraception. It is being used against the Church's doctrine. The so-called Würzburg Synod of the German Church went in the same direction and tried to cement this permissive, German interpretation of *Humanae Vitae*.

It might seem to those listening to us that this description of the gap between doctrine and practice is overly somber and pessimistic. Therefore, two quotations may help exemplify this thesis.

In a 1980 paper of the Federation of German Catholic Families (the largest organization of Catholic families in Germany), we read: "Probably seldom in the history of the Church has a situation occurred in which practice and people's convictions were in such flagrant contradiction to the doctrine of the Church in the field of marriage and the family. As to the question of contraception, especially after *Humanae Vitae*, nearly all couples made their own decisions in contradiction to the basic convictions and documents of our Church."

The second text, by the Basic Pastoral Questions Commission of the German Catholics Central Committee, the main lay organization of the German Church, was published in March 1982: "The gap between the obligatory ethical instructions of the Church and what people practice is nowhere as sensitive as in the field of sexual behavior. The disintegration in such central fields as the religious and sexual causes a situation of stress that leads inevitably to a loosening of bonds to the Church's doctrine in other fields as well or, at least, to considerable discomfort with the Church" (p. 335).

Following this, a German theologian stated: "The excitement about Paul VI's Encyclical is comparable to the excitement at a breach of the peace, not a positively engaged interest in the procedures of the Catholic Church" (p. 347). In these words, the demand for autonomous decision is loud and clear. This demand is nourished by modern theories of emancipation that consider documents of the Church's Magisterium on questions of fertility regulation as an inroad into the area of subjective rights. And, furthermore, they think they hear, in the voice of the crowd as a plebiscitarian majority, the *vox populi* with its *sensus fidelium* and the *vox Dei,* both in contradiction to the authentic Magisterium.

The "overwhelming majority" practices what has been "recognized as sure": dissent to the Church's teaching is the anticipation of future truth. In the opinion of these theologians, the Pope has not yet recognized the situation deeply enough, and they hope that in the future he will consent to the majority. Such is the opinion of leading German moral theologians who have free access to the media and whose books are published in great quantities by large Catholic publishing houses.

This situation changed little after the 1980 Synod and the Apostolic Exhortation *Familiaris Consortio*. The president of the German Bishops' Conference has clarified the meaning of the Church's doctrine, but guidelines are still drawn from the *Königsteiner Erklärung*, the Synod of Würzburg, and the changed practice of the faithful. This is done not only by theologians, parish priests, and the laity, but also by bishops (cf. Rottenburg, 1985).

Signs of hope: practical initiatives

In spite of this dark ideological background, we see hopeful signs on the more practial scene. Until 1980, natural family planning was almost unknown in Germany. During the 1980 Synod, many conversations took place among the bishops themselves and between bishops and lay people. These discussions led to many new beginnings. Through the Central Pastoral Office, Cardinal Höffner began a series of courses given by Dr. Flynn for teachers of natural family planning in ten major German cities. We, ourselves, began with Dr. Rötzer, who has since held many courses all over Germany. In more than one hundred lectures, we spoke about the Synod, its objectives, *Familiaris Consortio*, etc.

We were amazed how especially interested young listeners are in these questions. Many of them are open to the ideal of the family that is in accordance with the teachings of the Pope and the doctrine of the Church. For many women, natural family planning is a real liberation. They ask why it was not possible to learn all this earlier. In this, Germany has a lot to catch up on. However, we regret that natural family planning is taught mostly only as a method without considering its anthropological or theological aspects. This is one of the reasons why more than 50 percent of the participants dropped Dr. Flynn's courses. It is interesting to note that a great number of new natural family planning teachers are members of religious movements (Focolare, Equipes Notre-Dame, Schönstatt), so there is hope that their spiritual background will enter into their teaching. Since we were aware of this lack of anthropology as a basis, we held courses on it with Dr. Rötzer and published some articles on this subject.

The official German edition of *Familiaris Consortio* was accompanied by a commentary by a theologian who dialectically converted the Pope's teaching into its opposite. Therefore, it seemed necessary to us to publish a book with commentaries on the Exhortation. These commentaries by notable international theologians and experts in the humanities had been published previously in the daily *L'Osservatore Romano*. We were even able to help publish two other important books about these problems. In this way, scientific discussion in Germany can no longer ignore the Pope's teaching.

It is important to know this background if we want to understand the current situation in which German Catholics interpret the Holy Father's homilies from 1979 to 1984, and especially the last part from September to November 1984.

These homilies were printed regularly in the German *L'Osservatore Romano*, but hardly anyone took note of them. The only notable, worthwhile newspaper article (*Rheinischer Merkur*, Sept. 2, 1985) had the significant title: "Silence to a Message from Rome". In it we read: "Whereas, for instance, in America violent discussions are taking place concerning the Pope's teaching on marriage, no echo is heard in Germany up to now." Is this the result of the so-called anti-Roman trend (Hans Urs von Balthasar)? Is it the result of the fact that the Pope puts the anthropological question at the center of his reflections while this is treated as a secondary consideration in Germany? Natural family planning is becoming known but only as a method and as one among others with the same value. Nothing is said about the deeper motivation: everything is based on a positivistic, value-free position when facing this problem. In this system God's plan and his creation have nothing to do with the acts of real human beings. Here we find the explanation for the inability to see the anthropological and, at the same time, moral difference between contraception and natural family planning (cf. *FC*, no. 32).

All of this shows why it was extremely important to make a German edition of the Pope's homilies available in order to make them known. It was necessary to produce an inexpensive edition quickly without a commentary that would change the meaning of the message into its opposite, as had happened with *Familiaris Consortio*. We decided both to publish the homilies through a smaller publishing house in order to have a lower price and to write an introduction in conformity with the teaching of the Church. We also collaborated in the layout of the book. It was possible to find several persons who helped to finance the edition. A great deal of preliminary work went into it. Within a few months, we succeeded in publishing the three volumes of *Communio Personarum*. Volumes 1 and 2 contain the Wednesday homilies; volume 3 presents all the other statements of the Pope about marriage and the family.

After the papal visit in Germany, the 1980 Synod, and *Familiaris Consortio*, we have no doubt that something is moving in this field among couples and youth. They see and feel that it is a liberation to drop the pill and chemical means of contraception. Many begin to think after they have read the words of the Holy Father and the bishops.

Here we find the first steps for overcoming the gap

between teaching and life. It is necessary to recognize these steps and take care of them systematically. For this purpose, we have to spread knowledge about what the Church teaches. We need a pastoral program according to *Familiaris Consortio,* many good teachers for consultation on natural family planning, and a new family spirituality. This process of renewal in the spirit of the Church's teaching will take a great deal of time. Progress and a process that are rapid would do more harm than good. Much patience is needed. First of all, it will be necessary to develop a marriage-preparation program in the spirit of the Church, and to train priests according to the teaching of the Church. Much depends on the initiatives of the bishops. Couples and youth are awaiting these initiatives, which will also help renew Christian family life in the area of responsible parenthood.

THE POPE'S CATECHESIS ON "THE TRANSMISSION OF LIFE":

"Our Mission to Love and Understand the Truth of Life in the Face of Official Propaganda"

ALFRED AND MARIE MIGNON MASCARENHAS
(India)

Introduction

In this presentation, we have tried to highlight, as members of the Pontifical Council for the Family, our mission to love and understand the truth of life in the face of official propaganda against it and in the light of the various papal documents and catecheses and our own work experience in the family-life apostolate. "Since we are meant to be serving together with Christ in the mission of the Church here on earth, we are also responsible for seeking to understand the exact truth, for loving it, and for promoting it" (*RH*, no. 19).

It is in this "seeking to understand" the truths of the transmission of life that we the faithful are often found lacking in conviction and motivation. The tremendous propaganda, the need to conform with society, the fear of standing out against prevailing opinions, all this and more have damped our zeal and obscured the mission to understand and love the truth.

We must understand "the mystery of the sacrifice of himself that Christ offered to the Father on the altar of the Cross, a sacrifice that the Father accepted, giving, in return for this total self-giving by his Son . . . his own paternal gift, that is to say the grant of new immortal life in the Resurrection" (*RH*, 20).

We must understand "the mystery of the sacrifice of himself that Christ offered to the Father on the altar of the Cross, who, in return for this total self-giving by his Son, granted him immortal life in his Resurrection" (*RH*, no. 20). The *sacrifice of abstinence* as required by a couple who follow the teaching of the Church and use a natural method of family planning when needed cannot be underestimated. Are there any returns from the Father for this gift of obedience? We believe there are. However, first let us examine the various obstacles and myths encountered in the official propaganda and Catholic resistance to the Church's teaching.

I. Official propaganda

1. *Population growth* is dangerous especially because it is occurring mostly in poor developing countries.
2. The *basic resources* of the world such as food and water are *threatened* because they are being rapidly depleted by rapid population growth. Indeed the phrase *population explosion* is used to describe this situation.
3. *Contraception is necessary* if abortion is to be avoided; therefore, contraceptives should be made easily available.
4. Contraceptives should be provided *on demand* to any person irrespective of age or marital status.
5. Individuals have rights over their own bodies. Hence a woman can and should decide for herself when/if she

wants to abort; hence *abortion on demand should be made available.*

6. Science is making available more effective means to control fertility; hence we should take a modernistic view and use these technological means that are now so freely available.

However, to counteract official propaganda we have the following facts:

1. *Population growth*

Many experts have exploded the population bogey. Very specifically and applicable to all countries in principle, we have the arguments of an Indian expert, Professor Ashish Bose (president of the Indian Association for the Study of Population).

1. He asks whether it is possible to divorce family-planning programs from the broad social milieu of the Indian masses with their values attached to marriage, family, and children.
2. He believes that *Western norms* have eroded the solidarity of the family and weakened the institution of marriage.
3. He is convinced that the one-child model being advocated in the West and in China is *leading to a disaster and is bound to fail.*
4. He adds, "A society loses all dynamism if it has a zero population growth because in a few years the nation will be filled with old people, with very few young ones to offset the imbalance."

This, my friends, is no priest or religious speaking but an expert demographer of the Hindu religion.

2. Basic resources threatened

And yet we are told that there is more than enough to feed the world's population. As Mahatma Gandhi said, *"In this world, there is enough for every man's need but not enough for every man's greed."*

The Holy Father has called repeatedly on the rich nations to share their wealth and bridge the growing chasm between the haves and the have nots.

3. Contraception

The *myth* that wider availability and use of contraceptives would make abortion less prevalent has long been exploded. Statistics show that wherever use of contraceptives increases, abortion also increases.

Already in many countries, contraceptives are freely available, and in the United States *teenage pregnancy* and abortion have reached alarming heights. Simultaneously, *sexually transmitted diseases* have increased and are proving to be a serious health hazard in many countries.

Secular scientists agree that the *fertilized human ovum is genetically complete, with the whole human personality.* The mother offers shelter and nutrition, but the unborn child is a human being in whom growth and refinement are taking place (until he or she is an adult). The woman has a responsibility not only to her own body but to that of the helpless child, a whole person developing within her womb.

Technology is progressing and is being made increasingly available in the furthermost outposts of the world, *but the more effective the technology, the more powerful are its side effects or complications* (e.g., the contraceptive pill and the IUD). Technology cannot replace the oriental person's inborn love and respect for all that comes from nature, and in the West we see a definite attempt to seek out natural foods, preserve the ecology, and return, so to say, to nature.

4. *Transmission of life*

The Creator said, "Be fruitful and multiply, and fill the earth and subdue it." At a superficial level it would seem that man has done this. But at a deeper level we see that it is the earth that, in many instances, has subdued man, so that he is no longer master of himself. Man is precisely a person because he is master of himself and has self-control; otherwise there would be no difference between us human beings and the animal world.

Men and women have the power to give themselves to each other, but when they resort to "artificial means of contraception", they destroy the constitutive dimension of the person. Contraception deprives a person of the subjectivity proper to him and makes him an "object of manipulation", and so it is not man that subdues the earth but the earth and its products that manipulate and master man.

There is also no mutual self gift when a couple use contraceptives, which fully block the creative aspect and partly the unitive aspect of the conjugal act; being thus deprived of its procreative capacity, the conjugal act ceases to be an act of love.

Moreover, when a couple uses contraceptives, they cease to be "images made in the likeness of God", and they cease to exercise their greatest power of being cocreators with God.

To subdue nature, one must first understand nature and the natural rhythms of the bodies of men and women. Much of our knowledge of human reproduction comes from experiments with animals, and it is only recently that both the behavioral sciences and anthropology have shown the great chasm separating the two. Many of the conclusions that were and are still arrived at are based on the "genitality" of animals rather than on the "sexuality" of the human person.

This change in scientific understanding reinforces the change that the world (and not only Christians) must accept when *Humanae Vitae* speaks with authority of the human person as well as of his biology.

Now we also have scientific truth, namely, that love, as an emotion, is an impulse as real and strong as the coital impulse, which is the sole attribute of animals, in whom the biological instinct for sexual reproduction is independent of the higher centers in the brain. They do not have the capacity to love that we human persons possess, nor do they have the ability to form a relationship with genuine commitment.

II. Catholic resistance

This is widespread and influenced to a great extent by the media, contemporary opinion, and pressure. It is here that the Catholic laity, both scientists and lay married couples, have a very important role to play and can witness to the Pope's catechesis.

Humanae Vitae clearly outlines the moral difference between natural family planning and contraception: "In the former, married couples rightly use a facility provided them by nature. In the latter they obstruct the natural development of the generative process. It cannot be denied that in each case married couples, for acceptable reasons, are both perfectly clear in their intention to avoid children. But it is equally true that it is exclusively in the former case that husband and wife are ready to abstain from intercourse during the fertile period for reasonable motives when the birth of another child is not desirable. And when the infertile period recurs, they use their married intimacy to express their mutual love and safeguard their fidelity toward one another. In doing this they certainly give proof of a true and authentic love" (*HV*, no. 16).

Modern man shows a tendency to transfer the methods proper to "domination of the forces of nature" (*HV*, no. 2) to "*mastery of self*" (*HV*, no. 21). The latter in fact corresponds to the fundamental constitution of the person; it is indeed a "natural" method.

Let us now consider the factors involved in periodic sexual abstinence. First of all, we are dealing with a powerful physical urge, which is more difficult to quantify in humans than in animals. Although there can be no doubt as to the hormonal effects on the sexual drive both in males and in females, there are certain other factors affecting the drive for sexual relations, such as a conscious or unconscious need to dominate or to prove one's masculinity or (in the female) to bolster a sagging self-esteem and overcome threats of insecurity by being a desired sexual partner, which, refined, becomes the universal need to be loved and to love.

Couples helped to discover the rewards of periodic abstinence

The human being will finally perform that behavior which he believes will be rewarded in some way. The nature of the perceived reward may vary. It may be the satisfaction of seeing the spouse content, the alleviation of conscious or unconscious guilt, the attainment of financial gain or immediate physical gratification, or the assurance of a spiritual, heavenly reward in the distant future. Whichever it is or if it is a combination, the voluntary acceptance of a deprivation will generally occur only when there is perception of adequate reward.

Clearly then there must be a positive reward to compensate for the deprivation described earlier. Although there are others, probably the strongest consideration is a profound conviction, based on faith, that if there must be a limitation to the number of children, one may not tamper with the sexual act. Those who avoid contraception because they believe it to be a defiance of divine will have as their reward the enormous comfort of knowing that they are not transgressing the will of God.

If the certainty of their conviction is eroded by those who speak with theological authority and introduce doubt, this sense of reward is seriously undermined. On the other hand, the mutual adherence to that which one believes to be right and the tolerance of deprivation without external coercion can draw a husband and wife together in a union even stronger than one based on affection alone. Furthermore, through nonverbal communication, this conviction of one's ability to delay gratification is an attitude transmitted throughout the household and absorbed by the children. It is thus a true manifestation of conjugal love.

Freud stated that maturation consists of subjugating the "pleasure principle" to the "reality principle". If there is anything that threatens the existence of our culture, it is precisely this lack of maturation so defined, with the result that the quest for immediate gratification of various desires has led to millions of all ages, but particularly our youth, indulging in alcohol, narcotics, and various other dangerous chemicals or modes of behavior. But certain technological advances have had their side effects, for just as a muscle that is not utilized will suffer atrophy or disease and will be feeble when called upon to act, so an unexercised behavioral trait will wither from disuse.

And so it is that the ability to wait, to postpone gratification, has become somewhat of a historical relic. If postponement of gratification is not practiced in other areas of life, it will be most difficult to single out one area and demand tolerance of frustration in it, especially when the frustration is that of a constantly stimulated sexual drive. The culture that espouses the "instant-on" television because it cannot wait for twenty-five seconds of warmup time will be reluctant to delay sexual gratification for many days.

The practice of periodic abstinence can serve as a powerful deterrent to these destructive habits not only for those immediately involved but also for other members of their households.

Also, in the medical climate today the request for a physician's family-planning service and his response to the request will follow the lines of general expectations, on the part of both doctor and patient: something scientific, simple, rapid, and devoid of any kind of discomfort and something that only a physician can provide. Periodic abstinence has still to become accepted as satisfying these criteria, as indeed it can to a very positive extent. Hence a change of attitude is called for urgently.

Reflections on *Humanae Vitae* by John Paul II

In a series of talks given in his weekly public audiences in the summer of 1984, Pope John Paul II made some profound observations on the nature of the relationship between spouses in marriage, in which he spoke of the "language of the body".

Applying this series of reflections on *Humanae Vitae* and dealing especially with the moral norm in the fundamental structure of the marital act, he pointed out the inseparable character of its unitive and procreative aspects in behavior that is morally right.

Acts that are in conformity with this norm are morally right, while acts contrary to it are morally illicit. This interpretation of the natural law is taught by the Magisterium of the Church, although it is not literally expressed in sacred Scripture. John Paul II added weight to this magisterial interpretation by insisting that, in spite of its not being formally contained in sacred Scripture, it is contained in Tradition and, as Paul VI says, is "very often expounded by the Magisterium" to the faithful. It follows, therefore, that this norm is in accordance with the sum total of revealed doctrine contained in biblical sources.

Hence, says John Paul II, "it becomes evident that the above-mentioned moral norm belongs not only to the natural moral law but also to the moral order revealed by God." He urges every believer and every theologian to reread and ever more deeply understand the moral doctrine of the Encyclical, aided by his reflections. This must be the answer we give to those who do not acknowledge the authenticity of *Humanae Vitae*.

The spiritual dimensions of natural family planning can also be observed from the standpoint of the sense of mystery:

1. The mystery of the body of the spouse
2. The mystery of the fertile time
3. The mystery of the child
4. The mystery of the feminine and masculine
5. The mystery of God's Providence
6. The mystery of contemplation in action

For example, in defense of the use of natural family planning, an argument that is used is that illicit sexuality (i.e., when contraceptives are used) tends toward a gnostic separation of spirit and flesh, whereas healthy moral sexual expression ties soul and body together. How is it so?

In casual sex, the key factor is the individual's experience of his own sensual delight. The body of the other partner is an instrument for such pleasure but some other means can be substituted for it—hence the increase in artificial stimulators, homosexuality, masturbation, etc.

In married sex, the body of the other is loved as the incarnation of a unique personality—there are many possible females and males but one chosen spouse. It is, after all, quite a mystery that a body that one previously viewed as neutral, or merely a set of attributes capable of being rated quantitatively, becomes for the one in love a splendid, unduplicatable, beloved person.

The best answer to contraception lies in the example given by the many couples who loyally adhere to the natural method of family planning. These couples can demonstrate in their lives the positive advantages of responsible parenthood as shown in the practice of the morally acceptable method of periodic abstinence.

As every teacher of natural family planning knows from personal experience, clients repeatedly testify as to the positive rewards of practicing periodic abstinence, namely:

1. The wife feels she is no longer being exploited but is wanted for her own sake, thus gaining a new appreciation of her husband.
2. The couple appreciate the innate justice of a method that apportions equally the responsibility for the burden of family planning, requiring sexual discipline of both.
3. There is greater caring, confidence, and trust between

the spouses, combined with a more relaxed attitude and peace of mind and conscience.
4. The woman enjoys better health and gains self-esteem.
5. There is greater openness to pregnancy and the acceptance of more children, more love and concern for others.
6. Communication between the spouses is enhanced, leading to more harmony in the family.
7. Breastfeeding is promoted, leading to better health and psychological bonding for the child.
8. Finally, as fertility is preserved and their knowledge of it becomes precise and comprehensive, the couple enjoys a freedom that enables them to make truly informed choices about the number and spacing of their children.

Conclusion

The need of the hour is therefore that those actively engaged in the family apostolate throughout the world—the couples, youth, lay leaders, religious sisters, and priests—should constantly proclaim the values of conjugal love as perceived through the observance of the natural method of family planning. This constant repetition of the "good news of marriage and family life" is the best antidote to all official propaganda and those doubting clergy who mislead their flock by reflecting their own personal insecurity.

It is our task, as members of the Pontifical Council for the Family, to make the Holy Father's catechesis more widely known, to become enthusiastic apostles with an inner strength that is derived from our loving Father, through the grace of the Holy Spirit.

We remember our work with hundreds of priests, religious, and lay persons throughout India in courses on family pastoral theology and can reiterate that it has helped us to grow mutually in our faith and in support of the Church's teaching in the truths of the transmission of life. May we be given the grace to shine as witnesses of Christ here on earth as do the stars forever and eternally in heaven.

CONTINENCE AND FREEDOM IN CONJUGAL SELF-GIVING

RICHARD AND BARBARA McBRIDE
(United States)

We are certain that many of you are quite jealous of us right now, having wanted this topic on continence for your own assignment. Quite frankly, when we read our assignment our hearts sank! *Fifteen minutes* addressing the subject of continence before such an esteemed body of theological wisdom and experience was not what we would have chosen for ourselves.

But we came to realize, yet again, that the hand of the Lord directs us not always to the topic for which we may think we possess the greatest truth. Rather, he leads us to the topic through which he is waiting for us to discover new intellectual and spiritual understandings and zeal.

The "theology" we share is a theology of story, and our only footnotes are the moments of grace in our own life journey. We chose this method because it is precisely the way we minister to the real flesh-and-blood people in our lives. We first root our message in the truths of Scripture and the teaching of our Church; but we then cultivate and nurture those truths in the lived experience of our own matrimonial journey, inviting others to walk with us, discovering the Lord's call to them, and rejoicing in their desire and strength to live it.

Intimacy as a source of grace

We shall define intimacy as the love/communion/relationship of persons which is a deep sharing of selves, while still leaving their individual identities intact—in fact, those identities are actually enhanced, strengthened, and affirmed by their intimacy.

This love, which unites and deepens our human actions, is what we have been created for by our God. Intimacy is at the heart of any Christian spirituality; it is the call to establish a community of persons.

We are called by baptism to belong to one another, intimately in the Body of Christ; confirmation renews and directs this call to intimacy in the community of the Church for the sake of the world; Eucharist inserts us into the intimacy of Jesus and the Trinity—the supreme intimacy.

Matrimony is the sacrament which models for us—which witnesses and proclaims in tangible, available, recognizable form—that intimacy which transforms us from *persons* to *"a people"*, his people. What is essential to marital love is the intimacy of two persons who differ as much as any two individuals can and yet who enjoy a unity which is as inclusive as any unity can be. It is this intimate love which speaks of the covenant of matrimony, the binding promise of commitment, fidelity, permanence, and fruitfulness. And it is precisely this intimacy which models Yahweh's covenant with Israel, and Christ's love for his Church.

Intimacy then is the foundation of our matrimonial spirituality—specifically, an intimacy which is expressed, enhanced, renewed, and animated by and through our sexual relationship. The spirituality of marriage is incarnate. Our vows first pledged on our wedding day, and renewed each day through our continued presence, are a solemn promise to cultivate sexual desire for one another as a sacramental expression of our love.

Our sexual lovemaking is unitive and procreative. No one ever sees us making love, and yet all who meet us later experience the kind of transfiguration which has taken place within us—and through us to others. In that way we, in our love, are both cause—and effect—of the life of Christ in us. We are gentled, more tender, energetic, hopeful, willing to risk vulnerability, prayerful, awestruck again at the redeeming power of love—as lover and as beloved.

Just ask our children or the neighbors or the parish priest who looks out over his flock while preaching his Sunday homily. When are we most radiant, generous, and responsive to the community of the Church? It is when we have been reminded again of our belovedness through the power of sexual intimacy. And those mere moments of intercourse spill over their grace into the hours and days to follow, so that subsequent touches, laughter, tears, embraces, disagreements, fears, hurts, and healings are all colored by the marital intimacies which preceded them and the promised intimacies yet to come.

Continence and the freedom of self-giving

It is precisely into this fabric of matrimonial spirituality that true continence and freedom of self-giving can be woven lived, enjoyed, and proclaimed as yet another dimension of marital sexual intimacy. We are convinced that the ability and willingness to practice continence in a marriage are directly proportional to the quality of sexual love and commitment in that marriage. Those who love truly—and who know they are truly loved—have learned that love is not a *feeling but a willing*! We learn that love is benevolent; we wish for others the best of what we would wish for ourselves. We enjoy as our own fulfillment what is in fact good for the one we love.

We learn patience, forgiveness, other-centeredness. We learn self-discipline when we are truly loved and desirable. I learn self-mastery in order to be totally available to my beloved. And so I am able to reject the world's motto—"I want what I want when I want it"—and I choose instead to express my love and to be loved intimately and sexually but without intercourse if my spouse and I have prayerfully discerned that is where the Lord leads us for now.

(Actually, it is our firm conviction, through our understanding of the teaching of our Church, through our personal experience in our own lived sacrament of matrimony, and through the path we've journeyed with thousands of married couples throughout the world, that marital sexuality directs itself toward the transmission and nurturing of life, that sexual love is most fruitful when it is procreative as well as unitive. If we do not desire as many children as we can possibly nurture in our intimacy, then something is lacking in our intimacy. There is a definite ratio between matrimonial sexual pleasure and fruitful, benevolent, procreative love.)

Continence, then, is not simply a "giving up" or an empty self-denial or a withdrawal until the "right time" comes again. Continence is a choice to continue to live marital, sexual intimacy in a spirit of wonder at the divine power within us, to choose to love and to be loved in this way now for the sake of the Church and yet as a powerful sign of Christ's love for his Church. There is no decline of passion; there is simply a choice to express passion in other matrimonial ways.

Impediments

And so periodic continence too is a chosen response to the call to matrimonial spirituality. But the impediments seem to grow stronger each day. The impediments in society are so obvious: the allure of self-satisfaction; the use of sex as a solution for everyday problems; the use of sex in consumerism; the perception of sex as a tool for relaxation, recreation, inspiration, and self-identification; the absolute conviction that self-denial is only for the foolish or those on diets; the worship of the body; and the denial of the value of true spirituality—the list could go on and on. But, we propose that the most serious impediments to the appreciation of the positive contributions of periodic continence in matrimony for use as a Church come from within us—the Church herself. We list these as follows:

1. Lack of the development of a positive, affirming theology of matrimonial spirituality, which includes an appreciation of the spirituality of the sexual relationship, written in ordinary language for the understanding and uplifting of ordinary married couples.

2. A serious absence in priestly training and pastoral formation of the beauty and richness of the sacrament of matrimony as a prime sacrament in the life of the Church. Matrimony is still studied as a pastoral problem rather than as charism, gift, and grace.

3. A conviction on the part of most married couples that priesthood and religious life are far superior lives of spirituality and that married spirituality consists in following rules, contributing money and service, staying married, and raising children who remain in the Church. This conviction

is also deeply rooted in the priests and religious who "pastor us"—and so the belief continues from generation to generation.

4. Absence of an understanding of the parallels between vowed celibate love and vowed matrimonial love, each complementary to the other; each building up the body of Christ in a different but supportive fashion; both absolutely necessary for the continuing animation of the life of the Church. (It is also our conviction that when the holiness and spirituality of married sex are publically proclaimed in a believable way at the everyday, grass-roots level of our Church, when our married faithful are affirmed in their sexual relationship and are called forth to even greater passion and self-giving for the sake of the life of the Church, then vowed celibacy will flourish once again, and vocations to the priesthood and religious life will increase a hundredfold!)

5. Priests in the pastoral ministry who are insecure in their own vocation, priests who are insecure in their own sexuality and who are insecure in their own convictions with regard to *Humanae Vitae*—and so they avoid their responsibility to call couples forth to a renewal of their vocation to love and to the transmission of life and responsible parenthood.

Responses and conclusions

Our response to these impediments and our conclusions for this Council are to appeal once again for:

1. Theologies written for the understanding of those of us who are called to live them—and written in collaboration with couples who are learning to live them.

2. Increased support for movements and organizations which provide conversion experiences for the married.

3. Formation of seminarians and continuing formation of priests which focus on the charisms and holiness of matrimonial spirituality—as sexual, as unitive, as procreative, and as a symbol of Christ's love for his Church. This formation should be witnessed in practical, realistic ways by couples as well as through the usual intellectual pursuits.

4. Greater affirmation of the gifts of married people to the life of the Church and an ever-increasing willingness on the part of the institutional Church to allow and invite us to live our sacramental vocation with you in evangelizing the world. Holy orders and matrimony together will indeed be such a sign to the world of a Church alive and welcoming.

5. And lastly we who are married must call one another to strive to love more passionately, to pray more fervently, to sacrifice more generously, to forgive more readily, and to belong even more deeply to one another and to our Church. We must wrestle with our temptations to be superior and self-righteous; we must live matrimonial spirituality in all its aspects—from intimacy through sexual passion to intimacy through continence; we must challenge one another to self-abandonment, self sacrifice, self-discipline, and deep belonging, or else we are but clanging cymbals in an already too noisy world.

FERTILITY AWARENESS AND EDUCATION FOR CHASTITY

JEAN-MARIE AND ANOUK MEYER
(France)

Introduction

The word *chastity* is not fashionable. It is almost never used in catecheses and homilies. The term *fertility awareness* is used more but only in a technical context.

The unity of life

It must be well understood, even within our Christian ideas about marriage, that there are two different and complementary aspects.

First of all, there is a very "historical" aspect, connected with technical discoveries, regarding methods of fertility awareness. On the other hand, there is an underlying aspect that touches on the very nature of interpersonal relations: love implies self-giving. Now, self-giving implies the effort of giving oneself. Our conjugal life should unite these two viewpoints.

When we give talks on conjugal love, we must speak about the truth of conjugal love by suggesting to others that they discover this unity between the technical aspect and the deeper aspect of interpersonal relations. By speaking to others in this way, we try to "knock on the door of their hearts".

The reason for this unity

Our friends the Fortins spoke about the need for a catechumenate during the period of engagement. We feel that this is very useful. In fact, methods must always be placed in the context of conjugal chastity, and chastity in the framework of the whole of Christian living.

For this reason someone said that it is not a small thing to exercise responsible parenthood and that it is not possible if one is not in the state of grace.

Furthermore, recourse to the Eucharist and the sacrament of Penance is necessary so that Christian spouses will be able "to keep alive their awareness of the unique influence that the grace of the sacrament of marriage has on every aspect of married life, including therefore their sexuality" (*FC*, no. 33).

One must be aware that in this area it cannot be said that it is easy for some and impossible for others: it is difficult for everyone.

True liberation

One must know how to fight for the truth. At present, women's liberation is spoken of to a great extent, but often women have to manage by themselves with the pill or with abortion because of men's selfishness or lack of chastity. In concrete terms Saint Paul says that a man must love his wife "like his own body".

From the point of view that concerns us here, this could mean that the husband must love his wife's fertility cycle without burdening her with aggressiveness or selfish indifference.

Lastly, we believe that each couple, not the "masses", must be reached as far as possible.

Our world is full of coherent and convinced witnesses. We must "prove through our own lives" that the Church's message is really the good news.

THE RIGHTS OF THE FAMILY AND SOCIAL POWERS

LUÍS ALBERTO AND MARÍA DEL CORO PETIT HERRERA
(Spain)

Our topic

The report we are about to present is different from those made up to now, but it provides an occasion for everyone to receive some news.

With regard to the content of the Charter of the Rights of the Family, María del Coro could speak to you about her parish experience with care of the elderly and in a school for adults. I could speak to you about my experience as a university professor.

Again with regard to the content, we could speak to you about our participation in demonstrations against the laws on abortion and education in Spain as representing that type of social participation to which *Familiaris Consortio* refers (no. 44).

Profound changes

However, in considering the topic of the Charter of the Rights of the Family concretely, it would be more suitable to tell you that dark spots for the family are everywhere, based on the conclusions we have drawn from conversations following lectures we gave in many Spanish cities within the framework of regularly held Weeks for the Family.

In order to make an in-depth analysis of the Spanish situation with regard to the sociological and juridical aspects of the institution of the family, a series of studies and seminars were held, culminating in a public colloquium.

During that colloquium, the changes were studied which had taken place in the traditional family at a pace incomparable to the pace of those which had occurred in other institutions. At the same time, other cases of family cohabitation, which are no longer marginal, were also presented.

Legislation has changed with respect to the traditional model of the family based on stability in marriage, which was considered a contract between two heterosexual persons for the purpose of procreation and the socialization of individuals: that is, a family that had a given structure.

How this legislative change came about was examined in order to adapt to the new situation based on equality of the sexes, equality between legitimate and illegitimate children, and other values which are currently widespread: a situation in which the marital property contract is changed, etc.

Other sociological aspects were also studied such as mortality, fertility, and marriage, leading to the conclusion that in Spain, which has some of the lowest rates in Europe, there is a troubling situation. The fact is that in Spain we are going backward even before we get there.

Other points were made about the importance of the family as the basis for emotional and stable relationships (in fact, a person who lacks emotional relations will turn into a psychopath) and about the family as a source of food, educational resources, etc., and as the protector of children's responsible independence today in the face of radical authoritarianism and overprotection.

All of this takes place within an equalizing society which tends to eliminate differences between its various levels: that is, a uniformizing society.

With regard to the juridical aspects, it was noted that a definition of the family is lacking in legal texts at all levels. It is interesting that only the tax law regarding physical persons explicitly defines the family as based on marriage, thus making the Spanish saying right that the family is "those who stay inside the house when the door is closed".

The juridical order must be at the service of interests that deserve protection. Therefore, a statement of principles concerning the family as a social unit subject to certain rules cannot be evaded. The juridical order does not provide normative or identical protection for all possible cohabitating groups. In fact, those who want a type of union different from marriage do not have the right to demand norms that are the equivalent of those for real spouses. A contrary situation would be where those who join together for some reason would want the norms for partnerships to be applied to them even though they are only a union of those with similar interests. In fact, free unions are not dissolved with the same formalities as legal unions.

With regard to social-liberal democracies, all free spaces of liberty must be utilized in order to strengthen intermediate institutions vis-à-vis the temptations of any modern state to take advantage of citizens' dependence on the state in order to increase its power. This leads to the dual conclusion that, on the one hand, democracies are supported by the intermediate strata and, on the other, that society is lost without those intermediate institutions, of which the family is the first. As someone has said: "If humanity were ending in a cataclysm, the last man would spend his final hour looking for his wife and children."

The rights of the family

Following the International Congress of the Family, held in Madrid and concluded in March 1982, in which family organizations from fifty-one countries and different cultural, ethnic, and religious backgrounds participated, the United Nations felt the need for a Universal Declaration of the Rights of the Family. For this purpose, an International Secretariat was created, endowed with the required juridical characteristics for intervening better in international meetings, etc.

The International Secretariat, composed of twenty-six persons from nineteen countries, has been working since that date, first of all to draw up a draft text of the declaration and, secondly, for its proclamation.

The Secretariat's work is based on the fact that among the characteristic elements of the world, two are outstanding: a sense of the value of that social group called family, and acceptance of the need to form small social groups.

Although the family is the basic unit of society and, as such, its social rights must be recognized as independent of the familiar rights of the persons who compose it, still today the family cannot own anything or make contracts as a social unit. On the other hand, it is necessary for the family, which is a different entity from the persons who compose it, to have a special personality in cases where its material and moral interests are violated, as could happen with regard to food or to the diffusion through the mass media of subversive writings or images which threaten the family's physical or moral integrity.

The family is an entity whose personality and rights must be recognized—even if only in the terms of international declarations and treaties, and the laws of each country—and which must be seen as a social unit endowed with social functions without any detriment to the personal rights of the family's members.

It is sufficient, for example, to look at the reductionist views in some European laws on matters such as the right to life and the indissolubility of marriage—laws which exalt unlimited personal freedom—while fiscal laws in many cases penalize married persons compared with those living in free unions.

The draft text of the declaration obviously presents certain parallels with the Charter of the Rights of the Family even though it is not denominational. It limits itself to pointing out the less important negative aspects so that it can be acceptable to Catholics as well as other ethnic groups and cultures.

Perhaps the originality of the text lies in its division into two parts which consider the family rights of the person (the right to contract marriage, equality of rights, the right to life, the right not to be forced to use contraceptives, etc.) and the social rights of the family as a social unit (the right to employment, housing, health care, the education of children, social and economic protection, etc.).

In the text, an ethical content as the positive defense of family values prevails. It reflects the consensus achieved between the different denominations and the familiar bases of the different cultures so that the subject of the family could be positively updated and recognition obtained or, at least, so that a worldwide discussion could be opened on the family's social rights.

The itinerary

In view of its proclamation, subsequent meetings of the Secretariat were held in Madrid, Milan, Vienna, and Zagreb. From the February 1983 meeting on the occasion of the twenty-eighth session of the Commission for Social Development of the Economic and Social Council of the United Nations, during which the Secretariat contacted delegates from thirty-two countries, until the twenty-ninth session, held in February 1985, the long itinerary and the favorable environment being created in the United Nations with regard to the family were seen. It can be said that, after the twenty-ninth session, the commission seriously undertook the task of studying family questions, a task which it had begun hesitantly in February 1983.

For three days, the representatives of forty-nine countries, governmental delegates, observers, and nongovernmental organizations broadly discussed all the problems concerning the family based on the report presented by the Secretary General of the United Nations.

The report of the United Nations seminar held in Moscow (October 1984) on the family's role in the development process was also presented. During that seminar the possibility of a universal declaration on the family was raised, and the suggestion was submitted for study.

The family was referred to as the "natural and fundamental nucleus of society with the right to protection by society and the state" and as a "primary social unit". Among its functions, "the education of future generations", "the creation of moral, spiritual, and cultural values within society", "the sharing of efforts with other individuals, families, and social units", and "serving as a natural instrument for stimulating and channeling people's participation" were stressed. Due public recognition of the family as a factor in social integration was requested, and the direct relationship between the family and social well-being was stressed.

Therefore, the gradual shift in public opinion which was brought about in that twenty-ninth session in favor of a possible universal declaration on the family is important. It was a possibility that was not even considered at the previous session.

The Secretariat kept in touch with delegates from the different countries in order to foster a favorable environment for a declaration. In their interventions, the delegates from Italy, Canada, and Morocco as well as the ICCB, France, and the United States referred to the possibility and usefulness of this sort of action, although this outcome seemed premature "when there was still so much preliminary work to be done".

The official proceedings of the meeting report: "Other representatives referred to the possibility of an international strategy in favor of the family and suggested that the General Assembly ask the Secretary General for a solemn declaration or a universal declaration on the situation of the family and for the means that must be adopted on its behalf" (p. 76).

These proceedings are also evidence of the United Nations' concern for family questions and of the decision to create a committee of nongovernmental organizations to deal with topics related to the family. That committee held its preparatory meeting in the days preceding the twenty-ninth session.

Subsequently, in October 1985, a new meeting of this committee for the family took place with the objective of strengthening the family's role in the world and encouraging the formulation of a declaration of the rights of the family.

With regard to contacts with the Council of Europe, it must be said that family law occupies a modest position in that organization inasmuch as it tries to find harmonizing norms when diversity in the social fabric hinders identical solutions, as occurs in some areas of family law.

Up until the 1976 Brussels Conference, when harmonization was defined, only two agreements had been drawn up on this subject: one on adoption in 1967 and one on the juridical status of extramarital offspring in 1965.

The basic document of the 1977 Vienna Conference on Family Law does not change with regard to national systems but is superimposed on the search for greater harmonization.

As to conventions, in the CEDH the rights to life and to privacy are guaranteed by placing limits on the influence of public powers. It also deals with the right to contract marriage. Similarly, there are agreements on the repatriation of minors, the juridical status of illegitimate children, and the custody of minors, as well as a long series of recommendations.

The future

For those who work in pastoral care of the family, this echo, even if faint, at the United Nations and Council of Europe should help us persevere in our task.

At the same time, however, we must be aware that the law records only a part of people's aspirations. The rest must be sought in the sense of duty and responsibility each of us must take on over and above what contemporary society assumes.

LIVING A CHRISTIAN MARRIAGE

RON AND MAVIS PIROLA
(Australia)

Aspects of the question

Our theme is living a Christian marriage, with special reference to *Familiaris Consortio*, number 35, paragraph 3. This section is concerned with instilling convictions and offering practical help, and paragraph 3 focuses on the witness of married couples in this area:

> A very valuable witness can and should be given by those husbands and wives who through the joint exercise of periodic continence have reached a *more mature* personal responsibility with regard to love and life. As Paul VI wrote: "To them the Lord entrusts the task of making visible to people the holiness and sweetness of the law which unites the mutual love of husband and wife with their cooperation in the love of God, the author of human life."

You will note that our theme and the reference in *Familiaris Consortio* include *general* aspects of Christian marriage and one *specific* aspect—namely, the practice of periodic continence. This dual approach is appropriate because the two are related. It is hard to practice the specific (periodic continence) without the general (a mature Christian marriage), and yet the specific also helps achieve the general. Thus for Pope John Paul II, the witness in this reference is from those who "*through* ... periodic continence have reached a more mature personal responsibility", whereas in the full quote from Pope Paul VI the witness is by couples in the sacrament of matrimony *to* the "holiness and sweetness of the law" (*HV*, no. 25).

What we hear the Church stressing here is the importance of an integrated approach to sexual union, with periodic continence seen in the context of the whole sacramental relationship. This is also the basic theme of our presentation—that to "instill convictions and offer practical help" we need to take measures that deal specifically with the Church's teaching on periodic continence and at the same time to combine them with measures designed to improve the total witness of our sacramental marriages.

The real experience of marriage

But before we discuss those measures we would like to comment briefly on the witness of marriages in our society, which is a Western, English-speaking one.

Looking back over our twenty-six years of marriage, we can honestly say the most valuable witness that we experience in our lives is from married couples who do appreciate the essential link between the unitive and procreative functions of the sexual act. Sharing with couples like this makes us grateful to the Church for preserving a beautiful truth regarding the value of life and of our own marital union. We see couples who benefit in their married relationship from a growth in sensitivity, an absence of self-centeredness, a shared responsibility, and a growth in trust in each other's love and the part that God plays in that love.

They have an affection for each other that is attractive to others and a sense of peace and of purpose in their lives.

These effects flow over into their relationship with their children and with others. Their lifestyle is in sharp contrast to that of a society that distorts sexuality by emphasizing the act rather than the relationship, and self-centeredness rather than other-centeredness.

In our Western society, however, such witness is rare, and in addressing the question of living a Christian marriage, we need to understand the environment we live in.

Only a very small minority presently embrace the concepts of *Humanae Vitae* and live them out as part of an integrated spirituality. Of those Catholics who do practice natural family planning, many use it simply as a form of contraception that is free of side effects. Others practice it out of obedience to the Church. Because they have not integrated the practice with the mentality, they experience tension and are often angry toward the Church.

However, the majority of Catholics in our society don't follow the teachings of *Humanae Vitae*, and for many it seems no longer to be an issue. Factors that seem to reinforce their position include poverty, materialism, and consumerism, the increasing number of interfaith marriages (50 percent in Australia), and ignorance of the Church's teaching.

Furthermore, our clergy are reluctant to preach about something that for most doesn't seem to be working and for which they will be criticized. The overall effect is a resounding silence on this issue, a silence that diminishes the credibility of the teaching Church, even among her own people.

So against this background, how do we live a Christian marriage and witness to the Church's truths? How do we instill conviction of the value of periodic continence and offer practical help? We believe that we have to change from an approach that sounds negative and out of context to one that is clearly positive and is expressed meaningfully in the full context of the marital relationship.

The Christian animation of marriage

Our suggestion is that we explore three possible areas.

1. *The task of the Church*

The first is a coordinated and deliberate effort in the Church to *raise consciousness regarding the sacrament of matrimony.*

Until our married couples begin to reverence their life together as being a vocation—a call to take part in the life of the Church in a special way—they will have great difficulty in accepting and appreciating the truth of the inseparability of the unitive and procreative aspects of their union. A climate has to be created for the message to be heard, for the exercise of periodic continence to be seen as one jewel among many in the way a husband and wife live out their sacrament together. Like consciousness-raising in any area of life, what we are being called to has to be restated many times in very different ways before we begin to internalize its meaning in our lives.

This could be approached at two levels. First, at an *organizational* (hierarchical) level. Pope John Paul II has already given a lead in this area by the landmark decision to establish the Pontifical Council for the Family with a membership of married couples rather than of individuals who happen to be married. Some episcopal conferences have family commissions designed to affirm, support, and utilize the gifts of matrimony in the Church. But much more needs to be done at this level.

Second, on a *grass-roots* level, we need to develop opportunities that bring about a change of heart. Conversion experiences such as Marriage Encounter, and movements like Equipes Notre Dame and Focolare come to mind. Certainly, we know couples who through such experiences have been led to a new understanding of their life together and have begun to practice natural family planning as a result.

An effective way of raising consciousness of the sacrament of matrimony is by providing married couples with programs that allow them to share from their relationship as a couple. Nothing convinces a couple more of the graces of their sacrament than to see those graces in action—for example, in a marriage-preparation seminar or in a youth movement.

Furthermore, married couples need to be brought into the decision-making process of parish life, so that the perspective of couples can be recognized and clearly expressed.

We recognize the harmful effects of divorce on children and have no difficulty in appreciating the value of the marriage relationship in building the community on the domestic Church. We need to call on the value of that relationship for the wider Church.

In other words, the quality of the marriage relationship is important, and we need to affirm and reverence that as we do the other sacraments.

2. *A conjugal spirituality*

The second area that we think should be explored is the question of a *spirituality for married people*.

In his reflections on *Humanae Vitae* (Wednesday audience, October 3, 1984), Pope John Paul II refers to prayer, Penance, and the Eucharist as the principal sources of spirituality for married couples. This is an important truth, too easily glossed over by some who emphasize human responses to human problems. But it applies to all people, not just the married. We wonder whether the *specific means* of spirituality for married people lie in what is specific to their state in life—their sexual relationship. If the expression of aberrations in that relationship is morally bad and harmful to their life, then the correct expression of that relationship must be correspondingly morally good and beneficial.

The Church has always stated this, but the prevailing attitudes in the Church generally do not reflect it. We have a highly developed monastic/celibate tradition of spirituality that has enriched the Church for centuries to the extent that it dominates our attitudes, usually to the detriment of physical expressions of spirituality. Thus we talk about the "sign value" of the sacrament of matrimony and show concern at loss of that sign value through divorce. We don't show concern at loss of that sign value in huge numbers of marriages where the husband/wife relationship is externally no different from a brother/sister relationship—two good, caring people sharing their life together. The prevailing attitude is such that reference in ordinary conversation to a man as a good Catholic husband conjures up a mental picture of a caring man who provides for his family, is active in the parish, and who frequents the sacraments.

All these are part of being good and Catholic; only one of them is specific to being a husband. A good Catholic husband is one who loves his wife as Christ loves the Church, intimately and unconditionally. This love is not just emotional and spiritual, but physical as well.

The married relationship differs from all other relationships in the unique degree of sexual intimacy between the spouses. When the conjugal relationship is properly supported—in all its intimacy and sense of belonging—then periodic continence can begin to be seen as an integral part of that love relationship rather than just as a rule of the Church.

While we are deliberately stressing the central role of genital sex, we don't want to go to the other extreme and discuss it out of the context of the whole sexual relationship. Sexuality has to be discussed in the context of the total person and his relationships. I am never just a person. I am always distinctly male, and I discover my masculinity most effectively in my relationship with a woman (Mavis). We believe that it is this emphasis on an integrated spirituality of the total person that lies behind much of the Holy Father's writings on *Humanae Vitae*, especially his frequent references to "language of the body", "theology of the body", "prophetism of the body". We hear the Holy Father inviting us to broaden the horizon of sexuality to include the whole person rather than just genital activity. Natural family planning is a means of developing our complete understanding of this.

3. *Specific means*

The third theme we would like to underline concerns *specific ways to promote the proper use of periodic continence* in Christian marriage.

We think it is safe to say that people will not talk about this area of their lives except to their very close friends or relatives, or in special situations such as teaching natural family planning. Yet word of mouth and personal witness are the key means of bringing couples to natural family planning.

There is a need to set up occasions in which this subject can be explored in a constructive and supportive atmosphere

We believe nothing will happen until we start getting together those couples who are trying to live out the concepts of *Humanae Vitae*.

Specifically, we suggest that each episcopal conference experiment with a few selected parishes to develop a practical model that, once effective, could be introduced to other parishes. It is important that this approach start in a small way because a big diocesan campaign that is ineffective can be counterproductive. There are a number of advantages to this approach:

1. *Support.* At the very least, it will give encouragement to those practicing natural family planning who feel isolated and out of step with society.

2. *Enrichment.* It will provide a means for couples to help each other grow more fully into the life-giving concepts of *Humanae Vitae* and to apply them more effectively in their lives. If the parish priest can be involved in this process, then it will be of even more benefit to the couples and an enormous help to him in his pastoral work.

3. *Compassion.* We all experience failure in our lives. No couple lives out fully the concepts of *Humanae Vitae*. Therefore, members of such a group could be the most effective apostles of this message. This ministry of "like to like" would be an effective way of talking with realism, conviction, and, above all, acceptance and compassion to one's fellow Catholics.

4. *Listening.* Such groups of married couples could be effective vehicles for listening in the Church. We need to listen to the complex reasons why many of our good Catholics have sterilizations and use contraceptives. Furthermore, even

when the Church is actively listening, many people think it is not. Such groups could help to overcome this problem.

5. *Married people as a source of theology.* A further consideration is that groups such as these can become a resource in the Church. Married people are a source of theology. The Church is continually discovering new insights into the truth that it presents to the world. In the area of marriage, there is an unfolding of ideas from *Casti Connubii* through the *Church in the Modern World* (Vatican II), *Humanae Vitae*, and on to *Familiaris Consortio*. The general trend could be described as moving from a theology of actions to a theology of mentalities. The Church recognizes that special groups can have their own unique contribution to make to the faith of the whole body of believers. Married people have a unique and irreplaceable contribution to make. In fact, "the actual living out of the sacrament of matrimony is a necessary, if not sufficient, condition for a theology of marriage" (*FC*, no. 5). We need to encourage this process for the sake of the whole Church as well as for the sake of married couples and their families. We need to look for opportunities at all levels to bring married couples together to explore the meaning of Christian marriage. Such groups, working not in isolation but together with celibate clergy and theologians, can bring a richness to the Church's teachings.

In summary, to live a Christian marriage, we need to call our married couples to work with the rest of the Church in order to show the value of periodic continence in the context of a fully integrated love relationship, one that is physically, emotionally, and spiritually alive and growing.

THE CHRISTIAN FAMILY AT THE SERVICE OF RECONCILIATION

RODOLFO AND MARÍA VALDES
(Argentina)

Introduction

It has been said many times that the family is the basic unit of society. Having been created by God in his image and likeness, it must constitute a unit of life and love, just as God is love.

Personal experience and observation of our surroundings tell us that this ideal is not an everyday reality for the majority of families. This is due to marital disagreement, problems in relations with the children, an environment that is increasingly different from the one in which the parents were born, the influence of a materialistic, eroticized, and consumeristic society, and problems arising from poverty, lack of employment, and scarce housing. These are all fruits of a profoundly unjust society. But, above all, they are due to the sins of selfishness and pride—as described in *Familiaris Consortio* (no. 6) as "shadows of the family"—which easily lead family life into crisis.

What can we who work in pastoral care of the family do to make family life come closer to the Christian ideal?

1. Personal conversion and man's reconciliation with God

Undoubtedly, first of all, one's personal life must be renewed. Today one's life is not always lived with the rectitude and quality of behavior that should distinguish a Christian. (Could the expression "Look how they love one another . . ." apply today?)

Certainly, for many of our brethren, the evangelical message has not arrived, or it has arrived in a distorted way. Therefore, our first responsibility is an adequate evangelization and catechesis. In his Encyclical *Evangelii Nuntiandi* (no. 29), Paul VI insists on the reciprocal appeal which must be established between the gospel and man's concrete personal and social life: "Evangelization must include an explicit message, adapted to the various conditions of life and constantly updated, concerning the rights and duties of the individual person and concerning family life, without which progress in the life of the individual is hardly possible. It must deal with community life in society, with the life of all nations, with peace, justice, and progress. It must deliver a message, especially relevant and important in our age, about liberation."

In the Apostolic Exhortation *Catechesi Tradenae* (no. 19), His Holiness John Paul II adds that "the proclamation of the gospel must follow catechesis with the twofold objective of maturing the initial faith and of educating the true disciple of Christ by means of a deeper and more systematic knowledge of the Person and the message of our Lord Jesus Christ."

Therefore, personal conversion, as a result of evangelization and catechesis, is the basis of reconciliation in the family and in society, an indispensable premise. From each one's heart and life reconciliation will extend to the family, projecting itself onto relations between husband and wife, parents and children, young and old, the sick and the healthy. We know that each one of these categories today, in the interweaving of the family, has wounds and sufferings which call for the medicine of Christian reconciliation, as the Holy Father John Paul II explained in one of his many discourses.

2. Reconciliation in the couple

Today the family's stability, even its very foundation, is frequently threatened. Many couples marry with ideas that endanger the indissolubility of marriage, fidelity, or fecundity. These are fruits of the widespread propagation of materialistic models of life which are not Christian. (These remarks are derived from experiences with marriage-preparation courses.)

The Christian view about marriage is no more than a vague or even unknown concept, and a religious wedding celebration is only a traditional practice, a social custom to be kept.

Sanctification in married life requires feeling intensely the sacramentality of marriage, the concept that marriage is not between two but three persons, and the third one is Christ himself, who joins himself with and through the couple so that their married life will be holy and happy.

Living the Paschal mystery in conjugal life, the passage from death to life and from sin and division to reconciliation and unity has meaning at this time for only an elite group of Christian spouses.

Love is the root of the Paschal mystery because love is mysterious, and it is something which does not have meaning until it is given. The Paschal mystery is explained because the life to which Christ calls us through his Passion is a life of love. If life is love, and love is self-giving, then we do not grow in life or in love without sacrifice and without painfully shattering our selfishness. This is the meaning of the Paschal mystery in married life: Christ calls us to a life that is love, self-giving, and there is no love or giving without overcoming the sin which keeps us prisoners in ourselves. There is no growth in love without that pain. All pain is related to sin, to overcoming sin, being generous, and opening ourselves up to others.

The sacrament of matrimony means that the life of the spouses is to be a reflection of Christ's love. By committing themselves to one another, they promise to love one another with a love like Christ's love for us: this is the challenge.

However, if we compare our love with Christ's, we will feel that we are very far from that goal. But Christ himself, the Lord, offers us his strength so that spouses will be able to love one another as he loved us and sacrificed himself for the Church (Eph 5:25).

Many times one's love for the other will find a cross in the other's selfishness, indifference, sin, or limitations. Often spouses will have to learn to kiss that cross and learn to understand, accept, and forgive, and, on that cross, the Lord will be waiting for us.

He is also waiting for us with the strength of his Resurrection, which we can reacquire through the sacrament of Penance (*FC*, no. 58) and which we can nourish and maintain through the Eucharist (*FC*, no. 57). The Eucharist is the very source of Christian marriage. It represents the alliance of Christ's love with the Church, sealed with the blood of the Cross. In this sacrifice, Christian spouses find the root from which the conjugal alliance, fashioned from within and continually enlivened, is derived.

If spouses do not vibrate with the mystery of Christ's love, the rest of their married life and their function as parents will not have a solid base and will not be built on rock (Mt 7:24ff.; Lk 6:47ff.).

3. Reconciliation between parents and children

At times tensions arise in a family between parents and children. In the family, adults and young people, children and the elderly, interact and cohabit. Each one has different interests according to the different experiences each one has had. Many times conflicts arise out of different points of view; or because it is difficult for teenagers to accept their parents' authority; or because parents forget to soften their demands with love; or because the grandfather and grandmother, who are part of the family, cannot accept the changes—which are not really changes in values but only in attitudes—that are necessary in order to face the diverse situations of daily life.

At times parents consider their children as property, treat them like things rather than persons, and forget to help them develop as persons in truth, justice, and freedom.

For this reason, the encounter between the different family members is not always easy. Only love can help build unity in the midst of all the existing differences. This love means accepting the other person—father, mother, son, daughter, grandfather—as he is. This acceptance often means taking up a cross, and its weight can be lessened by experience aided by personal and family prayer, and by frequent Penance, as His Holiness John Paul II points out in *Familiaris Consortio* (no. 58). "Repentance and mutual pardon within the bosom of the Christian family, so much a part of daily life, receive their specific sacramental expression in Christian Penance." With regard to Christian spouses, Paul VI wrote in the Encyclical *Humanae Vitae*: "If sin should still keep its hold over them, let them not be discouraged but rather have recourse with humble perseverance to the mercy of God, which is poured forth in the sacrament of Penance" (no. 25).

The celebration of this sacrament takes on a special meaning for family life. Whereas through faith spouses discover how sin contradicts not only the alliance with God but also the alliance between the spouses and the family communion, they and all the members of the family are drawn toward the encounter with God, "rich in mercy", who, by infusing his love, which is stronger than sin, rebuilds and perfects the conjugal alliance and the family communion.

4. The family: a factor in the reconciliation of society

The family is the best place for experiencing reconciliation. It is the school where one learns to value the good in others and to share justly and generously. It is the place where we can learn to renew love, live our faith, and forgive again every day.

If families are capable of converting this into reality, they will be actively contributing toward creating a more just, more human, and more Christian society.

We cannot fail to quote the passages of *Familiaris Consortio* which show how the Christian family, a community at the service of man, can succeed in becoming the basis of a reconciled society. We make reference to numbers 63 and 64: "A daily effort to promote a truly personal community, initiated and fostered by an inner communion of love. . . ." "Love goes beyond our brothers and sisters of the same Faith because everybody is my brother or sister. In each individual, especially in the poor, the weak, and those who suffer or are unjustly treated, love knows how to discover the face of Christ and discover a fellow human being to be loved and served." "Another task for the family is to form persons in love and also to practice love in all its relationships, so that it does not live closed in on itself but remains open to the community, moved by a sense of justice and concern for others as well as by a consciousness of its responsibility toward the whole of society."

These reflections by the Pope invariably lead to the Gospel's teaching (Mt 18:15-17): "If your brother does something wrong, go and have it out with him alone, between yourselves. If he listens to you, you have won back your brother. If he does not listen, take one or two others along with you: the evidence of two or three witnesses is required to sustain any charge. But if he refuses to listen to these, report it to the community." This standard is applicable among members of the family, where it is practiced in order to be lived afterward in other institutions which are moved by the same ideals.

Saint Matthew also speaks to us about reconciliation in chapter 5, verses 23-24: "If you are bringing your offering to the altar and there remember that your brother has something against you, leave your offering there before the altar, go and be reconciled with your brother first, and then come back and present your offering." Between husband and wife and parents and children this search for true reconciliation will be best practiced where one learns how to live it in other circumstances and situations of social life.

Our bishops in Chile have understood things in this way. Facing the grave situation of hate and violence which is being painfully experienced in our country, they have called us to a mission for life and reconciliation with the motto: "Out of love for life, let us be reconciled in truth." This mission was opened by a Week for the Family, during which the families of Chile were invited to reconcile themselves from within beginning with the spouses, then parents and children, and then opening themselves up in order to seek the understanding and comprehension of other families.

It was a very meaningful experience for the thousands of families that participated in it. It indicated a path of hope in the midst of the conflicting realities we are living by making many, even from the same family, who had not spoken to one another or who could not tolerate one another because of their antagonistic political positions, share and fraternize.

For this reason with renewed faith we repeat the words of His Holiness John Paul II: "The future of humanity passes through the family" (*FC*, no. 75).

CHILDREN: CONTRIBUTION TO THE GOOD OF THE FAMILY

MARIJO AND DARKA ZIVKOVIC
(Yugoslavia)

We will share two points with you which we try to stress in our talks with couples and youth.

When we speak about loving and having children, we try to point out that our motivation for having children and for every action directed toward any of our children during our life together should be similar to God's motives for having created us and for doing or allowing anything to happen to us: that is, that God created us in the first place for ourselves. He wants us to exist and have a beautiful life, now and for eternity. Everything he does to us or allows to happen to us is done because he wants us to exist and have a happy, beautiful life full of satisfactions.

If we parents try to have such motives for everything we do to and for our children, we will be similar to God in our parenthood. All the other reasons for having a child and for doing something for a child—such as to add a new member to the human race; to have a child for the parents, the nation, or the Catholic Church; to add a future inhabitant of heaven; to give a new brother or sister to existing children; to have children who will help parents in their old age; or other reasons—are good, but all of them are included in the reason and motive we have described above.

By promoting that motive for having another child or for doing something for a child, we hope to clarify what is most important in our relationship with our children.

Another point we want to share with you is our position regarding the reaction, expressed or unexpressed, to the demanding moral teaching of Christ which is presented through the Catholic Church.

Often, when we explain Christ's teaching regarding contraception, natural family planning, or premarital chastity in its full sense, the reaction on the part of the audience is that it is not possible for some people. Sometimes in written reactions we find expressions such as: "Everything you have said is true and beautiful, but I have tried many times and was not able to succeed."

Therefore, we have developed the following answer: yes, perhaps it is not possible for me to follow Christ's full teaching now, being the person that I am now. But I can change myself. If I change myself through the ways the Church offers me—meditative prayer (we try to explain it convincingly), devout recitation of the Rosary, frequent and authentic confession (that we also try to explain), fighting vices by practicing the corresponding virtues, etc.—I will change myself sufficiently so that what is not possible for me today will be possible when I am changed and different.

I, Marijo, sometimes use this example. I ask the audience: As I am now (I weigh over 220 pounds), am I able to run around the soccer field three times without stopping? Obviously, as I am now, I cannot do it; but if I really want to, I can start to run around the field every day three times until I tire. In three to six months, I will be able to run around the field three times and still not be too tired.

We have shared this point with you because, for a long time, we have felt some sort of reaction from our audience which, if expressed, would be that Christ's full teaching is only for some people and not for all. By clarifying this point, we think that we show successfully that Christ's full moral teaching, as expressed by the Church, is for all people who really want it and are willing to use the instruments and methods which the Church is offering to all of us.